A GUIDE TO SANDWICH GLASS

VASES, COLOGNES AND STOPPERS

RAYMOND E. BARLOW

JOAN E. KAISER

PHOTOGRAPHS BY
  FORWARD'S COLOR PRODUCTIONS, INC.
  LEN LORETTE
  HUGO G. POISSON

EDITED BY LLOYD C. NICKERSON

BARLOW-KAISER PUBLISHING COMPANY, INC.

OTHER BOOKS BY RAYMOND E. BARLOW AND JOAN E. KAISER

The Glass Industry in Sandwich Volume 3
The Glass Industry in Sandwich Volume 4
A Guide to Sandwich Glass Witch Balls, Containers and Toys
A Guide to Sandwich Glass Candlesticks, Late Blown and Threaded
Barlow-Kaiser Sandwich Glass Price Guide

FORTHCOMING BOOKS BY RAYMOND E. BARLOW AND JOAN E. KAISER

The Glass Industry in Sandwich Volume 1
The Glass Industry in Sandwich Volume 2
The guides to Volumes 1 and 2 will contain:
    Whale oil and burning fluid lamps, with accessories
    Kerosene lamps and accessories
    Cup plates
    Lacy glass
    Blown molded glass
    Free-blown glass
    Pressed pattern tableware
    Salts
    Household items
    Cut, etched and engraved glass

A GUIDE TO SANDWICH GLASS
VASES, COLOGNES AND STOPPERS
First Edition

Copyright © 1987 by Raymond E. Barlow and Joan E. Kaiser

All correspondence and inquiries should be directed to

Barlow-Kaiser Publishing Co., Inc.
P.O. Box 265
Windham, NH 03087

in conjunction with

Schiffer Publishing Ltd.
1469 Morstein Road
West Chester, PA 19380

This book may be purchased from the publisher.

Try your bookstore first.

First Printing

Library of Congress Catalog Number
International Standard Book Number

Front cover: Photo 3152 Overlay Panel and Star colognes, c. 1860.

Back cover: Photo 3026 Loop vases with hexagonal standard and circular base, with dug fragment, c. 1850. Photo 3030 Bigler vases with octagonal standard and square base, c. 1850. *Courtesy of The Bennington Museum, Bennington, Vermont.* Photo 3147 Overlay cologne, c. 1860. Photo 3191 Wheel of stoppers, c. 1845.

Spine: Photo 3025 Six panel vase with octagonal standard and square base, c. 1850.

INTRODUCTION

A book that will guide you when you are in the process of buying or appraising Sandwich glass is the most important tool you can own. This book is one of a series of guide books that describes every type of glass that was produced in Sandwich, Massachusetts. It uses the original plates of glass photos and the identification numbers from Volume 3 of *The Glass Industry in Sandwich*, a larger book by the same authors. (Volumes 3 and 4 are available, and Volumes 1 and 2 are in preparation.) This makes cross reference much easier.

In order to make this series of guides compact and light in weight, the photos from Volume 3 have been divided into two smaller guides. This one contains the complete chapters on vases, colognes and stoppers. Another guide, available now, contains witch balls, covered containers, toys (miniatures) and the creations of Nicholas Lutz.

The extensive categorization and illustration of Sandwich glass should make this guide valuable for field use. The prices in this guide reflect the market at the time of publication. They will be periodically updated in a separate price guide available from the publishers.

WHAT IS SANDWICH GLASS?

It is simple to define Sandwich glass. It was all glass that was produced within Sandwich, Massachusetts, a town on Cape Cod that was founded in 1637.

Glass production came to Sandwich in 1825, when Deming Jarves built and operated an enterprise that became world famous. He called it the Sandwich Glass Manufactory. It was incorporated as the Boston and Sandwich Glass Company in 1826. During the sixty-three years it was active, the factory produced an average of 100,000 pounds of glass per week. Yet this production was only *part* of the glass that should be attributed to Sandwich factories.

In 1859, the Cape Cod Glass Works began to manufacture glass. For ten years, this second factory produced 75,000 pounds of finished glassware each week in competi-

tion with the Boston and Sandwich Glass Company. When the works closed, production once again started up in 1883 in the buildings that had housed the Cape Cod Glass Works, under the name of the Vasa Murrhina Art Glass Company. Because of manufacturing difficulties, very little of their spangle and spatter glass reached the market. However, the pieces that can be documented should be given Sandwich attribution.

There were several later attempts to manufacture glass in Sandwich after the closing of the Boston and Sandwich Glass Company factory in 1888. In that year, a group of glassworkers built a small glass works and called themselves the Sandwich Co-operative Glass Company. This venture lasted only three years, but its existence cannot be ignored.

The Electrical Glass Corporation started production in 1890, followed by the Boston and Sandwich Glass Company II, the Boston and Sandwich Glass Company III, and the Sandwich Glass Company. The Alton Manufacturing Company was the last to produce glass on this site. Its most notable product resembled Tiffany glass and was called Trevaise. Like its predecessors, the Alton Manufacturing Company was short-lived, and in 1908, glass was no longer manufactured in Sandwich. *But the glass made by these small companies deserves to be called Sandwich glass because it was made in Sandwich, Massachusetts.*

There were several other companies in Sandwich that worked on glass but did not make it. They cut it, etched it, engraved it, decorated it, and assembled it. The glass that they worked on, called *blanks*, was brought to Sandwich from factories in Pennsylvania. Regardless of what was done to the surface of this Pennsylvania product, *it cannot be called Sandwich glass.* Only glass that is shaped while hot can be attributed to a particular factory.

This book deals only with the glass that was manufactured in Sandwich and is therefore entitled to be called Sandwich glass.

VASES AND FLOWER CONTAINERS

1825–1908

Glass containers for holding flowers date back to Biblical times. With their use, flowers could be displayed in various arrangements, their beauty adding life and color to the surroundings. It is not surprising that when Deming Jarves began to produce glass in Sandwich, containers for flowers were included in his inventory. The earliest records from the Sandwich Glass Manufactory refer to *flower stands*. On December 31, 1825, flower stands with rings were listed by the man who tallied up each week's output in the company sloar book. This began a production run that continued for the sixty-two years that the Boston and Sandwich Glass Company produced glass through the halting of production by the Alton Manufacturing Company in 1908.

The records from that time make very clear that many of the glassmaking terms we use today are not those used at the time of production. For example, the word *lanthorn* preceded *lantern*. Creamers were called *creams*. The reason glass students have had difficulty in differentiating between *spill holders* and *spoon holders* is because they were originally manufactured as spoon holders regardless of their subsequent use. Similarly, a piece that would be identified as a *punch cup* by 1900 saw use as a *custard* in 1870. A new glass collector becomes understandably confused when he cannot distinguish among such various definitions and descriptive terms. The problem has been magnified by impatient researchers and writers who have arbitrarily assigned their own meanings to archaic terms and, in the process, failed to leave a trail that the serious student can trace.

There is no way of determining when the term *vase* came into use at Sandwich. The *Webster's Dictionary* from 1847 defines *vase* as "a vessel for domestic use, or for use in temples; as, a *vase* for sacrifice, an urn. An ancient vessel dug out of the ground or from rubbish, and kept as a curiosity." The 1864 edition adds " . . . especially a vessel of antique or elegant pattern used for ornamental purposes". Neither dictionary describes a vase as a holder for flowers, although present-day dictionaries do. By the time the 1874 Boston and Sandwich Glass Company catalog was released, *vase* was used in reference both to holders

for flowers as well as to ornamental pieces that were *not* designed to hold flowers, and *flower stands* were not mentioned. It is important to understand this change in nomenclature because we frequently look at the form of a vase and wonder how it ever held flowers without toppling over. Or we study a vase that has a design etched or transferred onto it and wonder how the busy design would fight with an arrangement of flowers. The answer is that every vase was not designed to hold flowers, but was meant solely to be used as a decorative ornament by itself.

We must agree that the term *vase* should not be used in connection with the word *celery*. An upright container designed to hold celery, pressed in a pattern or blown into a form that matches other table pieces, was called a *celery stand* or simply a *celery*, but never a "celery vase".

There was yet another use of the term *vase* in the glass industry, as an adjective describing a certain style of kerosene lamp. A *vase* lamp has a large glass bowl, or vase, into the top of which a metal can was inserted. A metal kerosene font was placed in the can, as shown in Volume 4, photo 4112.

The earliest "flower stands" that we have been able to document as Sandwich are free-blown trumpet vases and pressed pattern vases dating back to 1840. Regardless of their size, they are made up of several, separately-made units assembled and ingeniously held together by small wafer-shaped pieces of glass about the diameter and thickness of a quarter. In the early days of glassmaking in the United States, all glass factories heated their furnaces with wood. Heating the molten glass by wood limited the size of a piece of glass that could be pressed, because the glass did not maintain its temperature long enough to flow into all the crevices of the mold. When larger pressed articles were needed, the bases were pressed in one mold, and the upper units—candle sockets, bowls, lamp fonts, or vase trumpets—were blown or pressed into another. The units were joined by standing the base in an upright position, placing a hot wafer-shaped glob of glass on top of it, then placing the upper unit on the wafer and holding it until it adhered without support. Sometimes three units—a

The Enigma of Pairs

A pair of vases is worth more on the antiques market than two similar single vases, so the question inevitably arises—what constitutes a pair?

The answer depends upon the period in which the vases were made. Between 1825 and 1887, construction methods progressed from individually made, free-blown "flower stands" to pressed and Late Blown-molded perfect pairs. The earliest free-blown pieces varied considerably. No one, least of all the gaffers, expected them to be identical in height and diameter. If a vase overheated in the annealing oven and tipped slightly, or if a workman flared out a rim in a slightly different way, two similar flower stands were still thought of as pairs.

With the advent of pressing, the Boston and Sandwich Glass Company strove to make vases exactly alike, but their technique was not yet perfect. Separate upper and lower units had to be put together with a wafer. When one wafer was thicker than another, there was a difference in height. In most instances, no effort was made to line up the panels of pattern on the upper unit with the panels of pattern on the lower unit. Frequently, if two hexagonal vases are placed on a mantle with the straight edge of the lower units parallel to the edge of the mantle, the upper units appear to be askew. When a glassworker reworked a rim, there was often variation in height, diameter, and form as a result of the hand finishing. If the retail salesman found that the finish work drastically altered the forms of two vases pressed from the same molds, he might feel obligated to point this out to the retail customer. But in the final analysis, the judgment of the customer determined whether two vases were close enough in form and color to be considered a pair.

The Sandwich glass collector must use that same judgment today when considering the purchase of a pair of vases that date from the 1840–1860 period. *Consider as a pair only those items that match in color. Then determine whether the hand finishing has drastically changed the original shape, one to the other.* Auctioneers and dealers are inclined to hedge by saying, "A pair of similar vases", so it is still left to the buyer, as it was in the glass company showrooms, to use his own judgment. It is very difficult to assemble an identical pair, and this is the reason for the price difference between an exact matching pair and two similar single vases.

During the Late Blown Period, production methods had so improved that it was possible to blow vases in molds that left no mold marks. It was not necessary to rework them, so each piece was an exact duplicate of the previous one. It was expected that pairs of vases could be mated, so the Sandwich glass collector today should expect a pair of vases to be identical if they were manufactured during the last twenty years of the Boston and Sandwich Glass Company's existence. A study of the 1874 catalog will dramatize this fact.

base, a standard, and an upper unit—were joined to each other with wafers. The completed article was then carried to the leer to be annealed and the separate units were permanently held together. In the late 1830's when coal was used to heat the furnaces and higher temperatures could be maintained, the Boston and Sandwich Glass Company continued to use the wafer method of construction. It gave them great advantage over their competition at a time when costs of production were being watched very carefully. The years following the 1837 financial panic were lean ones, and molds were not replaced if they were still usable. The technology to mold a complete object in one piece existed and was being used by some other glass companies, but at the Boston and Sandwich Glass Company the wafer method was well entrenched. When a better grade of glass sand was discovered in 1845 and formulas were perfected to create new colors, a vast array of standards and upper units could be "mixed and matched" to make a variety of styles and color combinations.

There are many people who are not convinced that the Boston and Sandwich Glass Company continued to use wafers throughout their production years. The controversy compels us to document our research findings carefully. To date, our extensive collection of fragments dug from the factory site includes eighty-nine fragments of standards joined to an upper unit by a wafer. Our collection includes fragments dug by other historians, and there is not a single fragment of a vase with its standard and upper unit molded in one piece. This means that pressed pattern vases attached to marble bases also cannot be attributed to the Boston and Sandwich Glass Company, because we have never seen this type of vase with a wafer between the standard and the upper unit.

During our years of study, we have been fortunate to have access to many collections of Sandwich glass that were assembled at the time of production. General Manager Henry Francis Spurr brought pieces home directly from the works at Sandwich and the showroom in Boston. Lapham, Nye, and Lloyd are only a few prominent Sandwich employees whose descendants still have the pieces that were presented to their families, many with written documentation accompanying them. No pressed vases molded in one piece are included in any of these collections, with the exception of the few styles of very small vases that are nothing more than overgrown salts. *All of the pressed vases that we can attribute to Sandwich workers have wafers.*

A small collection of fragments dug from the site of the New England Glass Company in East Cambridge, Massachusetts, shows several lamps and candlesticks made in a one-piece mold. Patents taken out by or assigned to the New England Glass Company illustrate construction methods without the use of a wafer. A catalog of the New England Glass Company from the late 1860's shows pressed items molded in one piece, but we find no evidence that the Boston and Sandwich Glass Company or the Cape Cod Glass Company used that method. This does not mean that every piece with a wafer was made in Sandwich. The Mount Washington Glass Works joined units together with a wafer as did Pittsburgh houses. But it does mean that *a like item molded in one piece is not Sandwich.*

By the early 1860's, the manufacture of vases declined. For one, the Civil War curtailed production at both the Boston and Sandwich Glass Company and the new Cape Cod Glass Works. For another, kerosene had been discovered, creating a market for new styles of lamps to take the place of lamps that had burned whale oil or other types of burning fluid. The demand for kerosene lamps took precedence over the manufacture of vases and candlesticks, which faded away for almost a decade.

By the early 1870's, the Cape Cod Glass Company was closed, and competition from the Midwest glass houses forced the Boston and Sandwich Glass Company to concentrate upon the manufacture of thin-blown "bubble glass". The glass vases made during this period are well documented in the reprint of the 1874 Boston and Sandwich Glass Company catalog and in the Late Blown Ware chapter in Volume 4.

It cannot be emphasized too strongly that the Boston and Sandwich Glass Company did not excel in the manufacture of art glass vases. When this type of glass was being introduced by other factories, the Boston and Sandwich Glass Company was still concentrating on the very narrow segment of the market that would purchase threaded, acid-etched, and copper wheel engraved pieces for elegant dining. The Vasa Murrhina Art Glass Company, located on the site of the former Cape Cod Glass Company, tried to make and market art glass, and failed. The glass industry in Sandwich simply was not in a position financially to compete with other glass companies in new techniques such as Agata, Amberina, Burmese, Peach Blow, Pomona, or any other art glass form. Traditionally, these new methods were patented and assigned to a manufacturer by the inventor. Frequently these procedures were defended in the courts, but court records show that the Boston and Sandwich Glass Company did not become involved in any litigation resulting from art glass patent infringements.

Furthermore, the Sandwich Historical Society has a book containing minutes recorded at meetings of the American Flint Glass Workers Union, Local No. 16 in Sandwich. The book is dated 1879–1883. In the back of the book is a list of the items that were being manufactured at that time. The names of the items correspond with the names in the original price list that accompanied the 1874 Boston and Sandwich Glass Company catalog, proving that the company under General Manager Henry F. Spurr did not change its glass types and styles toward the end of its production years. The small amounts of Amberina and Peach Blow fragments that have been found in recent years on the surface at the Boston and Sandwich Glass Company site were from an attempt by Frederick S. Shirley to make art glass under the auspices of the Boston and Sandwich Glass Company II in 1896 (see Volume 4, page 82).

Finally, the old outdated furnaces were simply not capable of handling art glass. Vases appear to have been the only art glass articles made by the Alton Manufacturing Company in 1907. Called *Trevaise*, its identifying features are described in Chapter 17 of Volume 4.

THESE SIMPLE HINTS WILL HELP YOU IDENTIFY SANDWICH VASES.

The Boston and Sandwich Glass Company always used a wafer on pressed pattern vases. A like item molded in one piece is not Sandwich.

Each unit of a Sandwich pressed pattern vase is the same color, unlike candlesticks and lamps in which each unit may be a different color.

Pressed vases with marble bases were not made in Sandwich.

Art glass involving the blending and shading of two colors, such as Amberina, Burmese, and Peach Blow, was not produced by the Boston and Sandwich Glass Company.

Study the reprint of the Boston and Sandwich Glass Company catalog from the 1870's.

For vases in specific categories, study Chapters 6, 8, 11, 13, and 17 in Volume 4 of this series.

For many years, both the Town of Sandwich and the Boston and Sandwich Glass Company depended on bucket brigades to protect the Town and the factory against fire. Buckets and ladders were taken to the fire on this wagon, pulled by volunteers. In later years, the wagon was drawn by horses, as shown here. *Collections of Greenfield Village and the Henry Ford Museum, Dearborn, Michigan*

3001 FREE-BLOWN TRUMPET VASE

(a) Vase 10" H. x 3" Dia.

(b) Packing balls 2¾" Dia. 1840–1860

Certainly Sandwich made many free-blown vases, but unless there are family connections it is impossible to attribute a particular one. This vase belonged to the Tobey family in Sandwich. All of the family vases that have been made available to us have this type of base. The rims were reworked and turned outward, but the way the rim is folded cannot determine origin. It was at the discretion of the glassworker. The vase is made up of three pieces—the trumpet, the base, and the knopped standard. The trumpet is joined to the standard by a wafer, and another wafer connects the standard to the base. The packing balls were blown the same color as their vases, but appear to be lighter because they are so thin. For information on the use of packing balls, see Chapter 8.

3002 FREE-BLOWN TRUMPET VASES

(a) Taller 12¾" H. x 4⅝" Dia.

(b) Shorter 12½" H. x 4½" Dia. 1840–1855

Here are two of the best examples of free-blown vases from Sandwich we have ever seen. Each vase was made in three parts—the long trumpet, the standard, and the base. The base and standard were formed, then the trumpet was joined to the standard with the use of a wafer. The rim of the trumpet was folded to the inside and closed into a tight reinforcing ring. Even though there are slight differences in measurements, the vases are a pair. They were made from the same batch, albeit a batch that did not turn out to be the beautiful amethyst that was expected. Color expert James D. Lloyd wrote in his formula book dated August 7, 1868, that a really good amethyst is always clear. If soda is used it will give a brownish tint. The vases shown here are a marbling of amethyst and brown.

3003 FREE-BLOWN TRUMPET VASE
10" H. x 3½" Dia. 1840–1870

Free-blown "flower stands" of this type were made in almost every glass house during this period. Only the vases with glassworker family connections, documented as this one is, can be attributed to a specific factory. Any good glassblower would have the talent to duplicate this piece. It was made over a long period and was a staple in the industry. The trumpet and base were blown separately. The top of the standard is concave to accept a hot wafer of glass. The bottom of the trumpet is adhered to the wafer. In the base is an air bubble 1½" long. It is completely encased with glass. This is not a defect and does not affect the value.

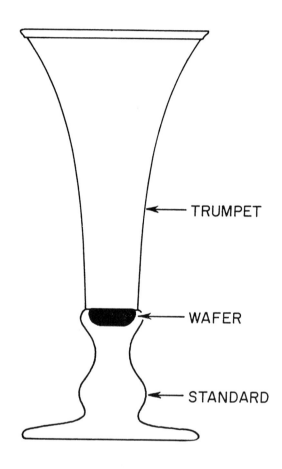

Fig. 3   The wafer is positioned inside the concave top of the standard and is covered by the bottom of the trumpet. It cannot be seen on the exterior of the vase.

3004 FREE-BLOWN TRUMPET VASE
9" H. x 4" Dia. 1840–1870

This vase came in many colors. The trumpet was also made to be inserted into a wooden base for cemetery use. Most of these blown pieces have their rims folded to the outside, away from the piece. This was known as *welted* in the industry. The trumpet was blown first and applied to the base when the base was still soft. If you find one at a sale with no documentation, it cannot be attributed to a specific glass house.

3005 FREE-BLOWN TAPPAN VASE
5¼" H. x 2¾" Dia. 1840–1860

This small vase is often sold by antiques dealers as a straw stem wine. There is no knop in the stem that would identify the piece as a vase in this small size. The base was made first, and the trumpet added to it. There is a rough pontil mark under the base where it was held when the trumpet was attached. If you find this vase without a pontil mark, it was not a vase made in Sandwich but a sherry made elsewhere in the 1920's.

3006 LATE-BLOWN TAPPAN VASE BLANK
18" H. x 6" Dia. 1870–1887

The Boston and Sandwich Glass Company catalog that was printed during the Late Blown Period carried photographs of clear glass before it had been engraved. These plain pieces were called *blanks*. The customer would pick out the piece that was wanted, and could chose from a variety of designs that would be copper-wheel engraved on it. The bottom of the trumpet was drawn out to become a plain stem with no knop. This style was known as Tappan by other glass companies, too. The plain trumpet inserted into a wooden base was used as a cemetery vase. When inserted into a metal fitting, it became the uppermost unit of an epergne.

3007 LATE-BLOWN DROP VASE
4⅞" H. x 2⅛" Dia. 1870–1887

This vase is a Tappan variant. It has the same blown trumpet, but it is connected by a button stem to a paperweight-shaped base made of solid glass. The Boston and Sandwich Glass Company called it a *drop flower vase*. It came in three sizes, all with the same proportions. A taller one would have a longer trumpet and a larger diameter base. Unlike similar vases produced by Pairpoint in New Bedford, the Sandwich one has a short peg between the button knop and the base, which is solid glass with no controlled bubbles. *Courtesy, Sandwich Glass Museum, Sandwich Historical Society*

3008 LATE-BLOWN VASES WITH PAPERWEIGHT BASE
(a) 7¾" H. X 4" Dia.
(b) 7⅞" H. x 4⅛" Dia. 1870–1887

According to his family, Nicholas Lutz made these for his wife Lizzie. The base is made up of pink, blue and yellow glass shaped into apples, pears and vegetables, and green leaves. These were encased in clear glass to form a paperweight base. The addition of a spool stem and free-blown upper unit completed each piece. This is a variation of the drop vase shown in the Boston and Sandwich Glass Company catalog, but the Lutz family pieces are much heavier than the thinly-blown production pieces. Records at The Bennington Museum indicate that these vases were intended for engraving. *The Bennington Museum, Bennington, Vermont*

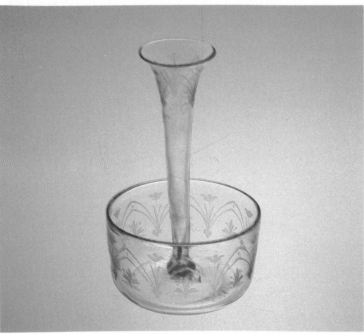

3009 FREE-BLOWN VASE FINGER BOWL
5¾" H. x 2¾" Dia. 1825–1835

Vase finger bowls are listed as such in the price list that accompanied a Boston and Sandwich Glass Company catalog that was printed in the 1870's. The piece shown here was made very early in the factory's history. Each unit was made separately. The bowl was blown, then reheated and shaped. A second man in the shop made the trumpet. While both pieces were still extremely hot, the trumpet was positioned inside the bowl, and the two units were fastened together by a glass wafer. The underside of the bowl has a pontil mark. If the piece was to have a design, it was engraved after the units were joined and the completed article was annealed.

3010 FREE-BLOWN VASE FINGER BOWL WITH LOW FOOT
5¼" H. x 2¾" Dia. 1835–1845

With no knowledge of their use, collectors call these pieces "small epergnes". But they were used as finger bowls, and a small bouquet in each vase added color to the table. The trumpet was fastened to the bowl with a wafer. Before the rims were fluted, they were folded for added strength. If it is Sandwich, it will have an unpolished pontil mark in the center of the foot. The engraved design on the trumpet does not extend below the rim of the bowl because the bowl was in the way of the engraving wheel.

3011 FREE-BLOWN GREEK BORDER SAUCER VASE WITH HIGH FOOT

6¼" H. x 4½" Dia. 1840–1850

This vase has wafers above and below the shallow plate. The top wafer holds the trumpet, and the bottom wafer connects the foot. The trumpet is only 4" high and holds a small bouquet of flowers. The saucer may have held after-dinner mints. Don't look for quality in these vases. They were made by the thousands to be used at each place setting on the dining table. Below the border design, clear and frosted panels alternate, with vertical lines bisecting the clear panels.

3012 FREE-BLOWN FERN TRUMPET VASE WITH BOWL

12" H. x 5½" Dia. 1860–1870

Sometimes a trumpet vase was combined with a high or low footed bowl to make an unusual vase. This vase is similar in shape to the Boyd vase shown on page 26 of the Boston and Sandwich Glass Company catalog from the 1870's. It is large enough to be useful and heavy enough to be durable. The trumpet was permanently attached when the piece was made. The fern and leaf design on the trumpet and the matching leaf design on the bowl were engraved after the piece was completed and annealed. Note how the design stops abruptly below the center of the trumpet. This is a common characteristic of Sandwich trumpets, whether used for vases or epergne units.

3013 LATE-BLOWN BOYD FLOWER VASE

8½" H. x 4¾" Dia. 1870–1887

Boyd is the name used by the Boston and Sandwich Glass Company for trumpet vases that could be detached from a compote-shaped bottom unit. The bottom unit was blown with a hollow base and standard that opens out to the center of the bowl, creating a socket into which the trumpet was inserted. The detachable trumpet made packing much easier for overseas and cross-country shipping. This piece was copper-wheel engraved with the letter "H" surrounded by a Number 2 wreath. It has been found in the family home of Sandwich glassworkers. The 1874 catalog shows two variations of the Boyd flower vase. This one appears on page 51. Another, shown on page 24, has a large knop toward the bottom of the trumpet, and the bowl is shallow. The number of fragments dug at the site indicate prolific production in clear and opal.

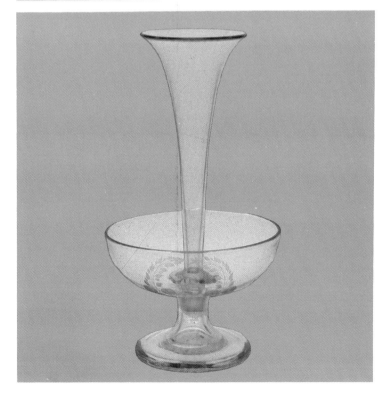

3014 FREE-BLOWN HYACINTH GLASSES
(a) Dark blue 8⅝" H. x 3⅝" Dia.
(b) Light blue 8" H. x 3⅝" Dia. 1830–1850
Hyacinth glasses are simply made. Their form is dictated by the growing habit of the plant. A hyacinth bulb is placed on the bowl-shaped rim so that only the roots come in contact with the water. The base was attached to the body when both units were of equal temperature, so a wafer was not needed. As a result of this crude method of assembly, the top is sometimes off-center. The edge of the base was folded to the inside. We have never seen hyacinth glasses with rigaree, scallops, fluting, or any other form of decoration. The dark blue color of glass A was used from the earliest days of production. It is often claimed that the Boston and Sandwich Glass Company made many things in blue because it was Deming Jarves' favorite color, but blue was the easiest and most inexpensive color to manufacture, and Jarves was a businessman. *Courtesy, Sandwich Glass Museum, Sandwich Historical Society*

3015 FREE-BLOWN HYACINTH GLASSES
(a) Shorter 9" H. x 3¼" Dia.
(b) Taller 9¼" H. x 3" Dia. 1830–1850
Because they were free-blown and finished by hand, the bowl that held the bulb varied in thickness, depth, and diameter. The height could vary as much as 1½". When you find hyacinth glasses in pairs, expect these variations. They may have been made by two different artisans working out of the same pot. Glass B was drawn out in height, accounting for the slightly thinner and therefore lighter colored body. There is a pontil mark underneath where the piece was held by a pontil rod while the top was shaped and the edge of the base was folded under. Fragments in quantity have been found at the factory site showing this wafer construction. Early records call these hyacinth *glasses*, not vases.

3016 FREE-BLOWN HYACINTH GLASS
6⅞" H. x 2¾" Dia. 1860–1887
This glass is from the collection of the descendants of Annie Mathilda Nye, a Boston and Sandwich Glass Company decorator. Many fragments of this base have been dug at the factory site, but many other glass companies also made this type of hyacinth glass. The Sandwich one has a rough pontil mark. It is rarely recognized as a Sandwich piece, which is understandable. Without documentation it cannot be attributed to a particular company.

3017 PRESSED LEAF VASES
11" H. x 6¼" Dia. 1840–1860
The mold for this pattern was most often used for a footed bowl. The flower-holding section of each vase was pressed into a bowl mold. It was then reheated and hand-formed into three upright sections, making three individual receptacles for the flower stems. The top vase section is held to the base with a wafer. The edge of the base has eight scallops. The leaf pattern is pressed on the inside of the base, and the outer side of the base is smooth. Leaf vases can be found in color, and the base was also used on footed Lacy dishes.

3018 PILLAR-MOLDED VASES WITH GAUFFERED RIM AND PRESSED MONUMENT BASE
(a) Deep flutes 11½" H.
(b) Shallow flutes 12" H. 1845–1860
Monument bases were made at both the Boston and Sandwich Glass Company and the New England Glass Company, and both companies are thought to have done a minimal amount of pillar-molding. These vases would be impossible to attribute without documentation, but the ones shown here have ties to Sandwich workers. To *gauffer* means to crimp or flute. A gauffered rim is made by reworking a rim that was perfectly round when it came out of the mold. Although both vases have seven flutes, they are not a pair. Vase A is shorter because the base overheated when the wafer was applied. As the upper unit was set in place the top of the base settled. Also the rim of Vase A was more deeply fluted than Vase B.

3019 PILLAR-MOLDED VASES WITH GAUFFERED RIM, PRESSED MONUMENT BASE AND CUT PUNTIES

(a) Taller, double wafer 12⅜" H. x 5¼" Dia.
(b) Shorter, single wafer 12¼" H. x 5⅝" Dia.
   1845–1860

We agree with Richard Carter Barret, former director-curator of The Bennington Museum, that this pair is perhaps the finest known both in design and workmanship. The difference in height is due to a production error. On Vase A, a wafer was applied to the pillar-molded upper unit, and another was applied to the top of the pressed lower unit. The two wafers were then joined together. After the vases were annealed, three punties were dished out of each vertical rib. Although the museum acquired each vase singly, they are well mated. We do no hesitate to call them a pair. *The Bennington Museum, Bennington, Vermont*

3020 PILLAR-MOLDED VASES WITH GAUFFERED RIM AND PRESSED HEXAGONAL BASE

(a) Round rim 10⅝" H. x 5⅝" Dia.
(b) Wavy rim 10¼" H. x 5¾" Dia. 1850–1860

Expect some variation in form and color when determining that two vases are a matching pair. The hand work necessary to complete these early items often caused them to be slightly different. Vase A is lighter because it was re-heated and drawn out more than vase B, thinning the glass. Vase B is closer in form to the shape of the pillar mold. It was not drawn out as much. The rim is thicker where the pillars meet the rim and thinner between the pillars, producing a wavy effect. We sometimes forget that they were meant to be used. When the vase was filled with flowers, the rims would not be visible. *Courtesy, Sandwich Glass Museum, Sandwich Historical Society*

3021 PRESSED TULIP VASES WITH OCTAGONAL BASE

(a) Dark amethyst, panels stop above peg extension
    10½" H. x 5" Dia.
(b) Light amethyst, panels continue to peg extension
    10" H. x 5¼" Dia. 1845–1865

Tulip vases were made by pressing the top and the base separately and putting them together with a wafer. This pair has eight panels in the top and base, but care was not always taken to assemble them in line. The peg above the wafer varies from ¼" to ½" high. Two types of molds were used at Sandwich to form the Tulip top. On vase A, the panels stop before they reach the peg. On vase B, the panels continue to the peg. To be considered a pair, they must have come from the same type mold. We have seen more than six shades of amethyst and large variations in height and diameter, making it almost impossible to assemble an identical pair.

3022 PRESSED TULIP VASE WITH OCTAGONAL BASE

(a) Blue-green vase 10" H. x 5" Dia.
(b) Green fragment 1845–1865

Tulip vases may be found in many unusual colors, such as the beautiful blue-green one on the left. The vase on the right is one of the most complete fragments found at the factory site. Only rarely can this vase be found with the scalloped rim flared out only slightly, which was the original shape of the mold. The mold marks will be seen all along the rim. Most vases were reheated and their rims were pulled out into the flower form. To be considered a true pair, two vases must be identical in color, must have come from the same mold, and their scalloped rims should have been reworked so that both vases are reasonably alike in height and diameter. This is why a pair has greater value than two singles.

3023 PRESSED TULIP VASES WITH HEXAGONAL BASE

(a) Amethyst 10¾" H. x 5⅛" Dia.
(b) Blue-green 10⅞" H. x 5½" Dia. 1845–1865

Tulip vases are seldom found with flaring hexagonal bases. Most of them have an eight-sided base to match the eight panels in the upper unit. But the Boston and Sandwich Glass Company's wafer method of production means that a collector can find any number of combinations, some of which may not be shown in this book. If *both* separate units can be identified as known Sandwich products, and they are joined by a wafer, the vase can be accepted as Sandwich without question. If *only one* of the units has positive Sandwich attribution, more thought must be given to the piece. It could be Mount Washington, because they also used wafers. *Vase B: The Bennington Museum, Bennington, Vermont*

3024 PRESSED TULIP VASE WITH GROOVED CIRCULAR BASE
10" H. 1845–1865

The Sandwich method of using a wafer to join separate units created unusual combinations. This pressed base blank is used on compotes. It is ½" shorter than the common octagonal Tulip base. The vertical grooves are molded into the upper surface of the base. Concentric circles are molded into the underside of the base on the example shown here, but some vases have been found without concentric circles. The wafer can clearly be seen between the two pressed units. Learn to identify the separate units and remember that any combination is possible and acceptable as Sandwich.

3025 PRESSED SIX PANEL VASE WITH GAUFFERED RIM, OCTAGONAL STANDARD AND SQUARE BASE
11½" H. x 4" Dia. 1840–1860

This is a good example of distinctiveness that was frequently created in glass. Note the wafer that holds the vase to the standard. The wafer was too large, and as the vase was pressed onto it the excess glass oozed out. The glass-worker quickly twisted the excess glass into petals, giving this piece individuality. In this side view, the edge of the wafer looks like rigaree. The mate to this vase does not have this petaled wafer, but they match in every other way, so are considered a pair. Their value should not be affected. If you want perfection, do not buy glass that dates before 1870.

3026 PRESSED LOOP VASES WITH GAUFFERED RIM, HEXAGONAL STANDARD AND CIRCULAR BASE
(a) Vases 10¼" H. x 4" Dia.
(b) Fragment 1840–1860

The Loop pattern is a popular one that can be found in full sets of tableware as well as in candlesticks. Six elongated loops make up the upper unit, but there are seven plier-marked flutes on the rim. The left vase has shallow flutes, but the difference is not noticeable enough to detract from them as a pair. As in all of the pressed pattern vases, the top was joined to the standard by a wafer. The fragment in the center is the largest in this pattern dug at Sandwich. It is from the former Casey fragment collection, now incorporated into the Barlow collection. Loop vases were also made in one piece, without a wafer, by the New England Glass Company, as were Loop vases with a marble base.

3027 PRESSED TWISTED LOOP VASE WITH GAUFFERED RIM, HEXAGONAL STANDARD AND CIRCULAR BASE
9¼" H. x 4¾" Dia. 1840–1860

When the glass was still hot, elongated loops were twisted about one-third of the way around. The vase has been reworked to the point that the mold mark is not visible. Six loops make up the body, but the rim was expanded to take eight flutes. The base, held to the top by a wafer, was made in a two-piece mold. It is a common base, but the twisted top is very rare. The standard is 1" shorter than the vase shown previously. It is proportioned to the lesser height of the top caused by the twist. Learn to recognize the basic form of a piece as it was molded, and you will be comfortable in attributing the hand-manipulated variations to Sandwich.

3028 PRESSED TWISTED LOOP VASE WITH GAUFFERED RIM, OCTAGONAL STANDARD AND SQUARE BASE
9⅝" H. x 5" Dia. 1840–1860

Here is the Twisted Loop upper unit joined to a 3⅛" square base. Before the rim was gauffered, its edge was folded to the inside. Unusual in these vibrant colors are the streaks of white running through the amethyst, creating a marble effect. This vase is in a private collection. We are grateful to the many collectors who have generously donated their glass and their time to this endeavor.

3029 PRESSED LOOP VASES WITH GAUFFERED RIM, OCTAGONAL STANDARD AND SQUARE BASE
(a) Green
(b) Blue 9¼" H. x 3⅜" Dia. 1840–1860

These two slender vases are smaller than most of this type. The base is 2½" square. Large quantities of elongated Loop pattern fragments have been found in the diggings and we have found that the Boston and Sandwich Glass Company used wafers even on the small pieces shown here. A greater variety of styles of lamps, candlesticks, and vases could be produced when their separate units were interchangeable. Sometimes wafers were used on stemware. Both top and bottom units of each vase came out of the same mold, but no care was taken to line up the mold marks of the top and bottom units of vase A.

3030 PRESSED BIGLER VASES WITH GAUFFERED RIM, OCTAGONAL STANDARD AND SQUARE BASE
11" H. x 4½" Dia. 1840–1860
The name *Bigler* can be found in a McKee and Brothers catalog from the 1860's. The vases are perfectly matched, and each vase is beautiful within itself. The slender upper unit combines nicely with the slender lines of the concave paneled standard. Each upper unit is joined to its base with the type of wafer most often seen on lamps with blown fonts and pressed bases. The two rows of pattern are separated horizontally by a bar and vertically by a groove. We place special emphasis on the horizontal bar because its high relief distinguishes Bigler from similar patterns. *The Bennington Museum, Bennington, Vermont*

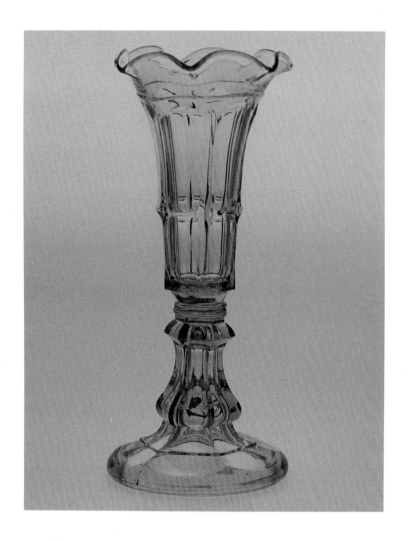

3031 PRESSED BIGLER VASE WITH GAUFFERED RIM, HEXAGONAL STANDARD AND CIRCULAR BASE
9½" H. x 4⅜" Dia. 1840–1860
For pieces that were made from two units, the pattern name refers to the upper unit. The gauffered rim was common at Sandwich. Don't let the number of flutes be a determining method of origin. They were hand formed at the discretion of the glassmaker. There may be six or eight panels of pattern pressed into the vase, and between six and nine flutes formed after the piece was removed from the mold. These early pieces were referred to at the time of production as *flower stands. Courtesy, Sandwich Glass Museum, Sandwich Historical Society*

**3032 PRESSED THUMBPRINT AND ARCH
VASE WITH GAUFFERED RIM AND
MONUMENT BASE**

12¼" H. x 4⅜" Dia. 1840–1860

If any vase can be called *masculine*, it would be this one. Its pattern lends itself very well to a straight-sided piece. There are six panels of pattern, and eight flutes in the rim. After the rims were reworked, they often dipped to one side. This is a characteristic of glass made in the 1800's, but it is uncommon today. The base is extremely heavy — the walls may be as much as ¾" thick. The monument base is often attributed to the New England Glass Company, but there is no question that it was also made by the Boston and Sandwich Glass Company. This pattern is often called a variant of Bigler. However, there is an area of smooth glass between the upper "thumbprint" and the lower "arch" in each of the six panels instead of the horizontal bar. We would prefer to call it *Two-Printie*, for reasons that will become clear in the following *Three-Printie* and *Four-Printie* photos. *Courtesy, Sandwich Glass Museum, Sandwich Historical Society*

**3033 PRESSED THREE-PRINTIE VASES WITH
GAUFFERED RIM AND HEXAGONAL BASE**

10¾" H. x 5½" Dia. 1840–1860

The term *printie* refers to the concave indentations. There are three such indentations running vertically in each of six panels. These panels were not lined up with the panels on the base, but the vases are as close a pair as you will ever find. Both rims were fluted to the same depth. The hexagonal base was used on lamps and occasionally on candlesticks. It can be seen on a candlestick on page 48 of Volume 4. These pieces had to have come out of the factory as a pair, and should be kept together. If separated, the two vases would be worth only two-thirds of the value of the pair. *Courtesy, Sandwich Glass Museum, Sandwich Historical Society*

3034 PRESSED THREE-PRINTIE VASES WITH HEXAGONAL BASE

10½" H. x 5¼" Dia. 1840–1860

Even though these are pressed, it is unusual to see a perfectly matched pair. The less they have been reworked, the better are the chances of finding an exact pair. Generally the top unit was placed on the wafer with complete disregard for lining up the panels or mold marks. This is a pair in perfect alignment. The rims were flared out slightly, thinning the glass and lightening the color. Three-Printie pattern and Bigler pattern both have vertical grooves (splits) between each panel, but no horizontal grooves. *Courtesy, Sandwich Glass Museum, Sandwich Historical Society*

3035 PRESSED THREE-PRINTIE BLOCK VASE WITH EXPANDED RIM, OCTAGONAL STANDARD AND SQUARE BASE

10" H. x 5" Dia. 1845–1860

Compare this pattern with the Three-Printie vases shown previously. In this vase, the addition of horizontal grooves between the three concave circles forms a block pattern. The upper unit that holds the flowers was made in a mold designed for the Three-Printie Block lamp font. That part which was flared out to make the rim of the vase would have been closed in to form the domed top of the lamp font. The knop beneath the pattern is part of the upper unit, and the wafer is below the knop. The 3" square base that works well when applied to a lamp is too small when used with this greatly expanded vase. When flowers are put in this piece, it is difficult to keep it from toppling over. It may have been an ornamental vase, not intended to be used as a flower stand.

3036 PRESSED THREE-PRINTIE BLOCK VASE WITH GAUFFERED RIM, OCTAGONAL STANDARD AND SQUARE BASE

9" H. x 3⅜" Dia. 1840–1860

The 2½" square base is the same one used on the elongated Loop vases in photo 3029, but the upper unit is a variant of Three-Printie Block. The mold was designed with ovals instead of round printies. The ovals were in the mold and were not the result of distorting round printies by reworking the vase. Six panels of pattern make up the upper unit, with seven gauffered flutes around the rim. The number of flutes can vary. *Courtesy, Sandwich Glass Museum, Sandwich Historical Society*

3037 PRESSED FOUR-PRINTIE BLOCK

(a) Vase with gauffered rim and hexagonal base
   11½" H. x 4½" Dia.
(b) Lamp 11" H. x 3½" Dia. 1840–1860

At first glance, this pattern looks like the one shown previously, but an additional fourth row barely a half block wide can be seen above the knop. This vase was one of the largest made in Sandwich for commercial purposes. The same molds were used to make both the vase and the lamp. The vase is taller because the glass was drawn up and out, elongating the top row of blocks. Expect minor variations in the hand-tooled rims. There are six panels of pattern molded into the vase, and six flutes gauffered into the rim. The rim could just as easily have had eight or nine flutes, depending on the whim of the gaffer. Both the vase and the lamp must be connected to their bases with a wafer to be considered Sandwich.

**3038 PRESSED FOUR-PRINTIE BLOCK VASE
WITH SCALLOPED RIM, HEXAGONAL
STANDARD AND CIRCULAR BASE**

10" H. x 5¼" Dia. 1840–1860

There are eight panels and eight scallops lined up over
each block. Scallops are part of the mold. Mold marks
sometimes can be seen on the edge of the rim, depending
on how much the glass was reheated and flared out. The
number of scallops cannot vary if the same mold is used
to make another vase. Gauffered rims are hand fluted
plain rims. There is no way to line up an eight-paneled
vase with a six-paneled standard. This is not a defect and
does not affect value. The usually graceful lines of Sandwich bases have been interrupted by the sharply-edged
band surrounding the standard. *Courtesy, Sandwich Glass
Museum, Sandwich Historical Society*

**3039 BLOWN MOLDED HEART VASES WITH
GAUFFERED RIM AND PRESSED HEXAGONAL
BASE**

9¾" H. x 4" Dia. 1840–1860

This pattern is common on Sandwich lamps, but occasionally the factory used a mold designed for lamp fonts and
adapted it to other pieces. After the glass was removed
from the mold, it had to be considerably reworked in order
to shape it into a vase. The pattern was lengthened, distorting it somewhat. The glass that would have formed the
dome of a lamp font was flared out and hand tooled into
seven flutes, even though there are six hearts around the
body. Do not mistake this pattern for the later Heart with
Thumbprint (Bulls Eye in Heart) pattern that was made
in Pennsylvania. In the Sandwich version, three hearts
have thumbprints in them, alternating with hearts that
have diamonds enclosed. The wafers can clearly be seen
in the photo. *Courtesy, Sandwich Glass Museum, Sandwich
Historical Society*

3040 BLOWN MOLDED HEART VASE WITH GAUFFERED RIM AND PRESSED HEXAGONAL BASE

9¼" H. x 4¼" Dia. 1840–1860

This vase appears to be the same as the last pair, but note how it was joined to the wafer. There should be a peg molded into the bottom of the upper unit. In the process of reshaping the glass from a lamp font form into a vase form, the peg, while in a molten condition, was absorbed into the body. This changed the height and appearance of the finished piece. If this vase was one of two and the only difference was the overheating of the peg, they would still be considered a pair. *Courtesy, Sandwich Glass Museum, Sandwich Historical Society*

3041 PRESSED ELONGATED LOOP WITH BISECTING LINES VASES

(a) Transparent green 4¾" H. x 3⅛" Dia. 1840–1850
(b) Fiery opalescent 4⅞" H. x 3¼" Dia. 1835–1840

The Boston and Sandwich Glass Company made very few small "flower stands" during the early years of pressing. There did not appear to be a market for them, and their scarcity today makes them very desirable. The hexagonal base is not hollow underneath—the vase was molded in one piece with no wafer, in the same manner as an egg cup or salt. The green vase is not as old as the opalescent one. There is more detail in the green vase. A reinforcing ridge can be felt along the inside of the scallops and, where the scallops come together, the ridge was machined smooth in the cutting shop. The dug fragments match the green vase in color and date. A similar item was also made in France by Cristalleries de Baccarat.

3042 PRESSED BALL AND GROOVE VASES

(a) Clear 5" H. x 3½" Dia.
(b) Amethyst 6" H. x 3¾" Dia. 1845–1865

If this vase had a name, it is lost to history. We are naming it *Ball and Groove* for obvious reason. By remembering the name, you will be able to differentiate easily between this Sandwich vase and a similar one made in Pennsylvania. The knob that protrudes out from the panels between the grooves is almost round. On the Pennsylvania piece, the knobs are egg-shaped, the smaller end at the top. Their other variations are minor. The vases from both areas were made in a mold with a scalloped rim. They were reheated and reworked, pulling the scallops up and out, much like the large Tulip vases. Unscrupulous antiques dealers sometimes buy these pieces with broken tops and have the tops cut off by a glass repair shop. The remaining portion is sold as a pressed salt.

3043 BLOWN MOLDED OVAL HOBNAIL WITH LEAF VASES

(a) Small pair 8" H.

(b) Medium single 10" H. 1850–1870

This style was made in three sizes. The hobnails are about the same size, but the small one has eleven rows of hobnails, the medium one has thirteen rows, and the large one (not shown) has sixteen rows. There are three long leaves that alternate with and overlap three short leaves. All of the vases in the Sandwich Oval Hobnail series have a pontil mark in the bottom where they were held as the rims were expanded. They were blown into the mold from the top down. This vase was also made in France. It can be seen in the book *L'Opaline Francaise au XIXe Siecle* with the hobnail bowl in a dark color and the trumpet and leaves in a lighter color. The ring separating the hobnails and leaves is less pronounced on the French piece. According to author Yolande Amic, the French vase can be found in a three-color combination. The Sandwich vase, however, was made only in a single color.

3044 BLOWN MOLDED OVAL HOBNAIL WITH LEAF

(a) Vases 8" H.

(b) Blown molded finial for newel posts and curtain rods 5¾" H. x 2¾" Dia. 1850–1870

Certain patterns lend themselves to multiple applications. When you are at an antiques show, keep your mind open to the surprise of finding unusual items in patterns you know to be Sandwich. There can be no doubt that, since the vase forms are documented as Sandwich, the finial is also. Finials can also be found in white and in green. We have a cologne in very light green, so don't limit your thinking to a particular color. The exciting part of collecting is never knowing what is in the next booth. The finial shown here was dug at the Boston and Sandwich Glass Company site.

3045 BLOWN MOLDED OVAL HOBNAIL VASE

5½" H. x 2¾" Dia. 1850–1870

This vase is very similar in design to the cologne in photo 3118. It is from the family of Charles W. Spurr, whose brother Henry was head salesman and then general manager of the Boston and Sandwich Glass Company. The top was reheated and expanded. The green rim was applied in the same manner that blue or red rims were applied to smoke bells. We have yet to see a piece in this pattern that is not extremely attractive.

3046 FREE-BLOWN VASES WITH BLOWN MOLDED CENTER

(a) Green with white Sawtooth (Mitre Diamond) center
   9" H. x 3½" Dia.
(b) White with green Oval Hobnail center
   9" H. x 3¼" Dia. 1850–1870

It is our opinion that these vases were not intended to have water in them. They are ornamental vases, not flower holders. Each vase is a composite of three distinct pieces. The center was blown into a patterned mold. The base was blown and fastened to the center with a wafer. The trumpet was blown with a wafer-like projection at its lower end, which was then attached to the top of the patterned center. On some of these vases, there is a hole through the center of the projection that allows water to enter the patterned center, but the hole is so small that it is impossible to clean the center. On some of the vases we studied, the hole was plugged up by excess glass from the trumpet, so only the trumpet would fill with water. Vase A is difficult to find, and Vase B is the only example of its kind we have encountered.

3047 FREE-BLOWN VASES WITH BLOWN MOLDED SAWTOOTH (MITRE DIAMOND) CENTER

(a) Blue 9" H. x 3½" Dia.
(b) Green 8¼" H. x 3½" Dia. 1850–1870

Although accurate measurements are given, they cannot be used as a method of attribution for pieces that have been free-blown or have had extensive hand finishing. These vases are alike to the top of the Mitre Diamond center, which was blown into a mold. The height changes by varying the length of the trumpet, which was free-blown. Before the rim of the trumpet was fluted, it was folded to the inside, making it a dirt catcher. Do not attempt to attribute origin by the direction in which a rim is folded. It was done at the discretion of the gaffer. *Courtesy, Sandwich Glass Museum, Sandwich Historical Society*

3048 ROSETTE
(a) Blown molded vase 5½" H. x 2¼" Dia.
(b) Blown molded cologne 4⅜" H. x 2⅛" Dia.
   1850–1870
Sandwich produced both a five-petaled and six-petaled Rosette pattern. These pieces have five-petaled Rosettes. The body of the vase was made from the same shape mold as the cologne, but the vase has a raised base. After the vase was removed from the mold, the top was reworked into its trumpet shape. *Courtesy, Sandwich Glass Museum, Sandwich Historical Society*

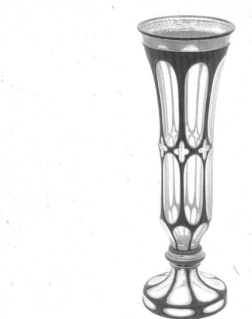

3049 CUT DOUBLE OVERLAY VASE PRESENTED TO ISAAC HOXIE
13¼" H. x 4½" Dia. 1856
Not many ornate Overlay vases were made for commercial purposes. Most were one-of-a-kind, to commemorate a specific occasion. This vase was one of a pair given to Isaac Hoxie on the day of his retirement. The base and trumpet were blown separately, and joined by a wafer. The design cut into the trumpet was well executed, but the base was not. The white layer of glass was too cool when it was blown into the pink, so it remained thick. When the design was cut into the base, too much of the white showed. Do not look for perfection in Sandwich Overlay —much of it is crude. A good way to study double Overlay is to look into the trumpet. The white middle layer can be seen from the inside, and from the outside the white layer appears as a white line separating the pink outer layer from the clear inner layer. The vase was gilded after it was cut.

3050 LATE-BLOWN VASE BLANK
9¼" H. x 5⅞" Dia. 1870–1887
The 1874 Boston and Sandwich Glass Company catalog lists this piece as "6065 plain vase". It can be seen on page 44 of the catalog in six sizes, ranging in height from 4 to 10 inches. Here, the claw feet curl outward, but they may sometimes be found curling inward. The top was reworked to provide a flat area to support the stems of the flowers. A berry prunt covers the pontil mark, but may not be present on every piece. The plain vases were called *blanks*, because they could be etched or copper-wheel engraved with standard factory designs as seen in the catalog or with wreaths and monograms as specified by the customer. This style was also made in opal, which was decorated with butterflies, flowers, or leaves. It can be seen with etched ferns in Volume 4, photo 4206. *Courtesy, Sandwich Glass Museum, Sandwich Historical Society*

3051 LATE-BLOWN VASE WITH ACID-ETCHED CASTLE TRANSFER PRINT

6" H. x 3¼" Dia. 1870–1887

This vase, made during the Late Blown Period, was listed by the Boston and Sandwich Glass Company as "6051 vase". It can be seen on page 44 of the catalog in four sizes ranging from 5" to 8". The claw feet curl outward, but occasionally pieces can be found with the feet curling inward. The feet and the lower ends of the reeded handles were applied to the body by pulling each ridge out until their appearance resembled scallop shells. The handles were drawn thin and attached at their upper ends. This vase has a castle acid-etched on one side and a small fern on the other. Don't dismiss a good piece of Sandwich glass because the design is unusual. The designs were purchased and could change from year to year. Many show European influence. This piece is in the family collection of descendants of James Lloyd and Hiram Dillaway.

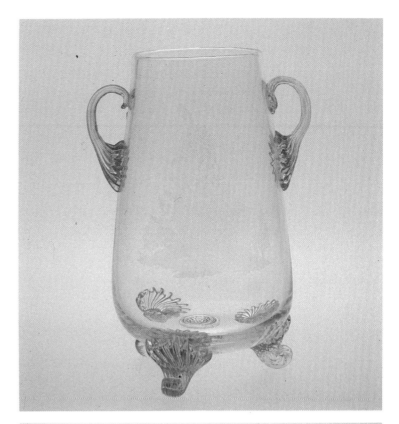

3052 BLOWN MOLDED OPAL RING VASE DECORATED WITH STORYBOOK CHARACTERS

7" H. x 2½" Dia. 1885

According to descendants of Boston and Sandwich Glass Company General Manager Henry Francis Spurr, it was his novel idea to copy illustrations from children's books onto glass. This Palmer Cox illustration of a frog riding a mouse is entitled, "A Morning Ride". It was taken from the book *Art in the Nursery*, published by D. Lothrop & Company in Boston, Massachusetts, in 1879. Spurr's family believed it was reproduced on glass about 1885.

3053 BLOWN MOLDED OPAL RING VASE DECORATED WITH STORYBOOK CHARACTERS

7" H. x 2½" Dia. 1885

This vase has a Palmer Cox illustration entitled, "Merrily, Oh!". It was copied from the same book as the vase above. It shows a rabbit being led merrily away by a fox, and the outcome was left to the reader's imagination. It is believed that many of these were made from early story illustrations. They are *not* transfer designs—each one was individually painted, so do not pass one by at an antiques show because the design is not familiar. Animals and landscapes painted with a rather heavy hand can be attributed with a fair amount of confidence to Edmund Kimball Chipman, whose work can be seen in Volume 4, photo 4259.

3054 BLOWN MOLDED DECORATED OPAL RING VASES

(a) Storybook characters 7" H. x 2½" Dia. 1885
(b) Raspberries from brier patch 8" H. x 3" Dia.
1870–1887

Several illustrations in the storybook *Art in the Nursery* depict the brier patch. Although the center vase is larger, and the design is painted above and below the rings, and there is no gilding on the rim, it has been identified by a Spurr family descendant as part of the same series. Note the dug fragment. It was made in the same mold as the larger vase and its color matches all of the vases perfectly. Many of these fragments are available in other colors, indicating prolific production in Sandwich.

3055 BLOWN MOLDED OPAL RING VASES DECORATED WITH RASPBERRIES

(a) Raspberries from brier patch
(b) Raspberries without thorns 8" H. x 3" Dia.
1870–1887

When we are able to authenticate Sandwich glass pieces as we were able to document the Spurr storybook vases shown previously, we can then attribute related pieces with accuracy. The vase on the right was found at an antiques show, but there is no doubt of its origin. Note the leaves below the rim, and the shadowy leaves in the background. There are minor variations on vase B, such as a lack of thorns and excessive ground cover. Slight differences reflect individual workmanship and do not affect the value.

3056 BLOWN MOLDED OPAL RING VASE DECORATED WITH APPLE BLOSSOMS

6⅞" H. x 2⅝" Dia. 1870–1887

Ring vases with floral designs depicting flowers, shrubs, and trees indigenous to the New England area were commonly produced by the Boston and Sandwich Glass Company. It was not unusual to see Sandwich artists in the meadows and fields of Cape Cod painting animals and plants in their natural surroundings. In the decorating room, the designs were simplified and adapted to glass. Vases with hand-painted designs that do not depict local nature cannot be attributed to Sandwich. In addition to the gilding on the rings, this piece has narrow gold lines delineating the floated blue ground. *Courtesy, Sandwich Glass Museum, Sandwich Historical Society*

3057 BLOWN MOLDED OPAL RING VASE DECORATED WITH QUEEN ANNE'S LACE

4⅝" H. x 1¾" Dia. 1870–1887

Ring vases were made in several sizes. This is the smallest. The delicate tracery of wild flowers combined with a pastel yellow ground provide a pleasing design for this diminutive vase. Many times only the center of the vase is painted, but on this piece the blade of grass begins beneath the bottom rings. The artist carried the design to within ¼" of the rim. Designs painted with a very light touch show the influence of Edward J. Swann, who came to Sandwich late in 1872. Swann expanded the decorating department of the Boston and Sandwich Glass Company and added variety by searching out local talent having different painting techniques. *Courtesy, Sandwich Glass Museum, Sandwich Historical Society*

3058 BLOWN MOLDED OPAL RING VASE DECORATED WITH BUTTERFLY

6¾" H. x 2⅝" Dia. 1870–1887

This type of ring vase with four gilded rings and a completely decorated center was made in quantity at Sandwich. This vase would have been described in their catalogs as having a *floated center*. The green ground color was floated on only between the rings. The butterfly and its landing area were hand-painted. A transfer (decal) was not used on this piece, although transfers were used on a great many. There is greater value in a vase painted completely by hand than in one on which color was added by a transfer. Ring vases were also hand-painted at Mount Washington. *Courtesy, Sandwich Glass Museum, Sandwich Historical Society*

3059 BLOWN MOLDED OPAL RING VASE DECORATED WITH BLUEBIRD AND DRAGONFLY

8" H. x 3" Dia. 1870–1887

White opal glass was often tinted to make other soft colors, so the color of the vase blank should not be a determining factor in identifying a Sandwich piece. This bluebird is a good example of the detail originating from the Boston and Sandwich Glass Company decorating department. The bird is taking off to chase the dragonfly. Friedman Miller, a skilled decorator and naturalist, went to the fields and forests of Cape Cod to paint scenes in their natural colors. His work was copied by the other artists in the decorating room, who adapted his designs to vases, flower pots, and even smoke bells. The ferns and foliage completely surround the vase.

3060 BLOWN MOLDED OPAL RING VASES DECORATED WITH GREAT BLUE HERON
5⅞" H. x 2⅜" Dia. 1870–1887

The great blue heron is the most common design painted on ring vases. This type of decorating was initiated by the Smith Brothers when they worked at Sandwich. It was continued by them at the Mount Washington Glass Works in New Bedford and at their own decorating shop in New Bedford, where they utilized Mount Washington blanks. Ring vases were also made by Samuel Bowie in New Bedford and by Gillinder and Sons in Philadelphia. Based on fragments dug at Sandwich, we are able to document three variations of the heron design. In this first variation, the green reed shows between the heron's legs, passing behind and over his body. There are no brown cattails. Other variations appear in photos 3061 and 3072. If the vases are a true pair, the birds will face each other.

The Smith brothers. Harry A. Smith is on the left and Alfred E. Smith is on the right. *Courtesy, Sandwich Glass Museum, Sandwich Historical Society*

3061 BLOWN MOLDED OPAL RING VASE DECORATED WITH GREAT BLUE HERON
7¾" H. x 2½" Dia. 1880–1887

This vase was painted by Annie Mathilda Nye, who worked at the Boston and Sandwich Glass Company from 1880 until the last of the decorating work was completed in 1888. This variation has heavy stalks on each side of the heron, and brown cattails. The salmon background color was *floated* on. Some decorated vases had floated centers and were plain at the top and bottom. Some had floated tops and bottoms and were white between the rings.

3062 BLOWN MOLDED OPAL RING VASE DECORATED WITH ELK TRANSFER PRINT

7" H. x 2½" Dia. 1870–1887

The elk, the rocks in the foreground, and the water are part of the transfer print. The clouds and sky were touched up by hand to "dress" the piece. The color above and below the rings and the gilded lines on both sides of the rings were painted on by a decorator called a *liner*. The fragment matches the vase in shape, but its base has six indentations. Both types were made in Sandwich.

3063 BLOWN MOLDED RING VASE WITH ACID-ETCHED BIRD TRANSFER PRINT

6" H. x 2⅜" Dia. 1870–1887

Sandwich made very few pieces commemorating a particular holiday. The words "A MERRY CHRISTMAS" are on the branch behind the bird's feet. The tree is bare of leaves. There is a vine of five-lobed leaves along the right side of the branch and across the bottom. The rings are etched, as is the border design at the top and bottom. These vases were not expensive. They were packed on their sides in layers protected by a layer of straw. Packing balls were not used. If, in transit, the rings of one vase touched the rings of another, they were not likely to break.
Courtesy, Sandwich Glass Museum, Sandwich Historical Society

3064 BLOWN MOLDED OPAL RING VASE DECORATED WITH CHARIOT TRANSFER PRINT

7" H. x 2½" Dia. 1870–1887

The Boston and Sandwich Glass Company catalog price list describes this piece as "colored top and bottom, black figure vase". The picture of a chariot drawn by two horses was acid-etched into the white glass blank, and the lines were filled with black enamel. The black line on each ring was put on by a decorator called a *liner*. After all the color work was completed, the vase was sent to the decorating kiln. Study page 59 of the catalog reprint for other black figure designs. The chariot design was also used on a cone shade shown on page 66 of the catalog.

3065 BLOWN MOLDED RING VASE WITH ACID-ETCHED CHARIOT TRANSFER PRINT
7" H. x 2½" Dia. 1870–1887

Many clear glass ring vases were made and acid-etched in Sandwich. They are not often recognized by inexperienced collectors. Study the "black figure" designs that are on the opal ring vases shown in the factory catalog on page 59. Don't be afraid of slight variations in designs, because the prints were purchased and changed from year to year. The Greek Border variation etched around the top and bottom is an unusual touch. It can be found on an opal decorated flower pot in the catalog. Original catalogs are invaluable in the documentation of a company's product. We carry a copy with us when we shop for Sandwich glass.

3066 ETCHING PLATE, FIRST DESIGN
1870–1887

A glass etching plate at the Sandwich Glass Museum has several designs that were used on clear and opal articles during the later years of production. This chariot design is the one most often found and can be seen on the ring vases shown previously. Note the Greek Border on the horse's girth and the stars on the cape. The etching plate originally belonged to the Russell family, two generations of whom had a member working at the factory. *Courtesy, Sandwich Glass Museum, Sandwich Historical Society*

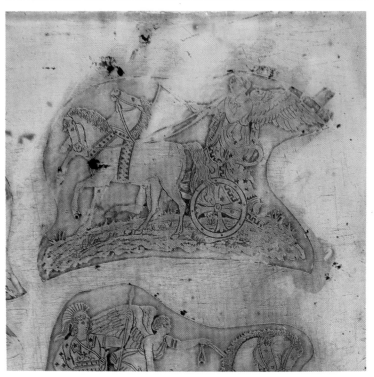

3067 A SECOND DESIGN ON ABOVE ETCHING PLATE

All of the designs on the etching plate are related in some way. A similar winged goddess is holding the reins. Note the stars on the clothing. The chariot is bordered with a Roman Key design, used frequently on Late Blown Ware (see Volume 4, Chapter 11).

3068 THIRD DESIGN ON ABOVE ETCHING PLATE

Here is a single horse whose rider is wearing a cape embellished with stars. A study of the 1874 catalog shows that the decorated items were not described according to design. The opal vases were listed as *black figure*.

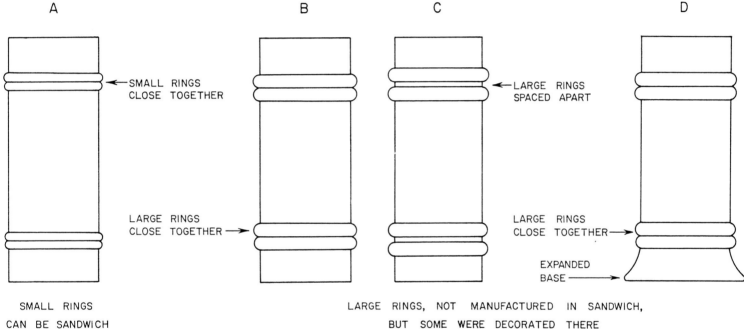

Fig. 4   All of the vases we have been able to document as having been *manufactured* by the Boston and Sandwich Glass Company have small rings, as shown in illustration A, although other glass companies also made them. Note the size of the rings in proportion to the vases. The large-ringed vases were not manufactured in Sandwich and most of them were not decorated in Sandwich. The small percentage of large-ringed vases that found their way to Sandwich were blanks that were purchased from other sources by Edward J. Swann and Charles W. Spurr, both of whom operated decorating shops after the Boston and Sandwich Glass Company closed. Do not attribute a large-ringed vase to a Sandwich decorating shop unless it is accompanied by irrefutable documentation. A vase with the expanded base shown in illustration D was found at the site of Spurr's decorating shop. It can be seen in Volume 4 on page 128.

Fig. 5   Only two types of bases have been found on ring vases *manufactured* by the Boston and Sandwich Glass Company. Family pieces and dug fragments show that some vases have a bottom that is perfectly flat, as shown in the illustration on the left. Others have a recessed base with indentations made from cleats in the bottom of the mold in which they were blown. The number of the indentations may vary, but each indentation is trapezoidal in shape — wide toward the outside of the base and narrow toward the center. Other glass houses also made these two types, so there is no way of identifying Sandwich ring vases by examining the bottom.

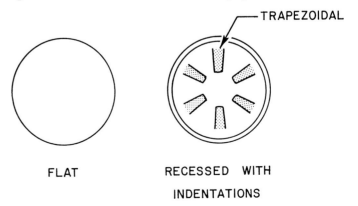

3069 PRESSED OPAL VASE DECORATED WITH AUTUMN LEAVES

4¾" H. x 2¼" Dia. 1875-1887

To reliably attribute Sandwich glass, we must have more than one method of proof. Even this strikingly simple vase can be traced two ways. First, it was passed on from the family of Annie Mathilda Nye, who worked in the decorating department under Edward J. Swann. Second, all of the fragments dug at the site of the factory have the stems of autumn leaves twisted together, even if there are only two leaves. The light pink background was applied first. After the leaves were painted, the color was made permanent by firing the piece in the decorating kiln. The leaves vary in color from piece to piece.

3070 PRESSED OPAL VASE DECORATED WITH WHITE VIOLETS

4" H. x 2" Dia. 1875-1887

These pieces are often mistaken as being made by the English firms of Stevens and Williams, or Richards. Many of the flowers native to Sandwich are also grown in England. This is one reason why identification is difficult. The leaves of this white violet plant provide us with a clue. Note the shading in the leaves to give them depth. Their similarity to work done by Edward J. Swann tells us that an artist under his tutelage painted this vase. The color of the glass can be determined by looking into the vase. The blue background is a floated color. The rim is gilded.

3071 PRESSED OPAL CYLINDER VASE DECORATED WITH GREAT BLUE HERON

6" H. x 2¾" Dia. 1875-1887

Straight-sided vases without rings are not shown in the 1874 Boston and Sandwich Glass Company catalog, but the heavy cattail reed between the legs of the bird is an identifying feature that can also be found on ring vases made by the company. A sprig of wheat is painted on the other side, echoing the painting on the front. The rim is gilded. Learn the styles of blanks that were used at Sandwich. Any of the designs that can be authenticated as Sandwich can be found on any authenticated style of blank. This includes blanks for cone shades, gas globes, finger bowls, and flower pots. *Courtesy, Sandwich Glass Museum, Sandwich Historical Society*

3072 PRESSED OPAL VASE DECORATED WITH GREAT BLUE HERON

4¼" H. x 2⅝" L. x 1¾" W. 1907–1908

All of the long-legged birds painted in Sandwich or New Bedford are great blue herons, although some resemble storks and are often sold as such. Designs were painted from nature, and there are no storks along the Massachusetts coast. This is a third type of heron design found on the fragments dug at the factory site. The reeds are heavy and look like cornstalks. Note the poor quality of the floated blue background and the lack of detail. It is easy to tell that Edward J. Swann was not in charge of *this* decorating department! We believe this piece was a product of the Alton Manufacturing Company in a last attempt to manufacture glass in Sandwich.

3073 BLOWN MOLDED OPAL VASE DECORATED WITH GREAT BLUE HERON

9⅛" H. x 4¾" Dia. 1880–1887

This vase is usually attributed to the New England Glass Works in East Cambridge, and to the Smith Brothers in New Bedford. However, family records from Sandwich decorators and fragments dug at the site prove that the Boston and Sandwich Glass Company produced this shape *after* the Smiths left Sandwich. Annie Mathilda Nye painted this vase. She was born in 1860 and began working at the factory in July 1880, according to Emma Gregory's diary. This vase was made in one piece out of opal glass. The color was painted on, but the white of the heron and the water lilies is the color of the glass. Only one heron is on each vase in all of the heron series. A pair of vases has one heron on each vase facing each other. If the herons are facing the same direction, the vases are two singles and should be priced individually.

Annie Mathilda Nye, decorator.

3074 BLOWN MOLDED OPAL VASE DECORATED WITH RASPBERRY SPRIG AND INSECT

7⅛" H. x 3¾" Dia. 1875–1887

The shape of this vase cannot be found in the 1874 Boston and Sandwich Glass Company catalog, so it is not often recognized by collectors. *All* the shapes shown here and in subsequent photos have family documents that tie them to Sandwich. Also, look for fine detail in Sandwich vases, such as the insect coming in for a landing from the left and the barbs on the stem. The background is a soft pastel, and the base is painted black. Gilding separates the two colors. Another gilded line is on the rim. *Courtesy, Sandwich Glass Museum, Sandwich Historical Society*

3075 BLOWN MOLDED OPAL VASE DECORATED WITH DAISIES, BUTTERFLY AND LADYBUG

10" H. x 3¼" Dia. 1875–1887

Note the ladybug on the blade of grass to the right. The butterfly with full wing expansion is on a daisy to the left. Sandwich artists were able to capture a moment suspended, very much as a high-speed camera can freeze living action today. A band of gilding separates the background color from the black base, and the rim of the vase is gilded. After being blown into a mold, the opal vase blank was annealed, then sent to Edward J. Swann's decorating room. After the artist completed his work, the vase was fired in a decorating kiln to permanently fix the color. *Courtesy, Sandwich Glass Museum, Sandwich Historical Society*

3076 BLOWN MOLDED OPAL RAISED FLOWER VASE

10" H. x 5" Dia. 1870-1887

By today's definition, this vase would be called "milk glass". It was made by blowing the hot glass into a mold. The glass conformed to the shape of the mold, so that the leaves and flowers can be felt on the inside in reverse. The sculptured effect leads many to believe this was a product of Pennsylvania's Phoenix Glass Company, but three variations of this piece can be seen in the Boston and Sandwich Glass Company catalog reprint on page 60. A cigar holder of similar style belonged to the family of James D. Lloyd, Deming Jarves' color expert. Other than cigar holders and vases, the company generally did not employ this type of "puffy" construction.

3077 BLOWN MOLDED OPAL RAISED COLORED FLOWER VASE

10" H. x 5" Dia. 1870-1887

The background color is brushed on between the raised flowers and leaves. We have found it in blue as shown here, and in lavender and brown. The white border and floral pattern stand out in relief, giving a cameo effect. A gilded line surrounds the rim, and the ring above the band of leaves is gilded. The catalog also shows this piece in reverse—the flowers are decorated and the background was left white. This third variation was called "opal raised painted flower vase". Sandwich was *not* noted for using white enamel. When white was needed as part of the design, the blank would be made from white glass.

3078 PRESSED CHRYSANTHEMUM LEAF VASES

(a) Large 10⅛" H. x 4" Dia.
(b) Medium 8⅜" H. x 3¼" Dia.
(c) Small 6⅛" H. x 2⅝" Dia. 1875–1887

There is always an exception to the rule, such as these pressed vases molded without the use of a wafer. They are similar in construction to a goblet. This pattern was the last commercially made at the Boston and Sandwich Glass Company. Very few early patterns of tableware have matching vases. There are six leaf panels. Each leaf is slightly different in shape. The row of dots in each stem is in no way related to a chrysanthemum leaf in its natural form. Sometimes the stem is gilded or ruby stained. The color adds greatly to the value of the vase. *Courtesy, Sandwich Glass Museum, Sandwich Historical Society*

3079 PRESSED CHRYSANTHEMUM LEAF VASE

7" H. x 7½" Dia. 1875–1887

The bulbous shape of this piece resembles vase styles of the early 1900's. The wide base made flower arranging easier. It would not tip over even if the design of the arrangement leaned heavily toward one side. We know of no other glass company that made this pattern in clear glass with or without gilding or staining. However, both styles of vases can be found in Chocolate glass, which was manufactured in the Midwest after the Boston and Sandwich Glass Company closed and sold its molds to Jones, McDuffee, and Stratton in the Spring of 1889 (see Volume 4, page 19). This piece is sometimes called a carafe, but its short, wide neck makes it almost impossible to hold for the purpose of pouring. *Courtesy, Sandwich Glass Museum, Sandwich Historical Society*

3080 SPANGLE VASE

6½" H. x 3¾" Dia. 1880–1887

Fragments of spangle glass are found in quantity at the Boston and Sandwich Glass Company site and at the Vasa Murrhina Art Glass Company site (see Volume 4, Chapter 8). Much of it was produced, but very little reached the market because of its inherent tendency to crack. Most spangle glass came from Hobbs, Brockunier and Company, where it was manufactured under a patent issued to William Leighton, Jr. on January 29, 1884. John C. DeVoy's patent for Vasa Murrhina was issued only five months later. During this time period, patents were granted regardless of their similarity and were later fought out in the courts if either patentee was unhappy. Note the simplicity of this piece — no attempt was made to flute the rim or apply a base or handle. Pieces that were reworked can be attributed to the Wheeling, West Virginia firm.

3081 BASE OF ABOVE VASE

The metallic flakes are mica that was coated with silver. A gather of glass that was to become the inner layer of the vase was rolled on the marver to pick up the flakes. This gather was then reheated and blown into an already formed outer layer of clear glass. Note the heavy concentration of flakes on the bottom. This was caused by an uneven pickup of flakes when the gaffer rolled the gather on the marver. The uneven distribution caused stress between the layers, making these pieces impossible to rework without cracking at the old, inefficient Sandwich furnaces.

3082 VASA MURRHINA VASE
5⅞" H. x 4⅝" Dia. 1883–1884
This is an excellent example of the Vasa Murrhina glass that was made by the Vasa Murrhina Art Glass Company at the site of the Cape Cod Glass Company. It has an outside surface of gold and magenta, and is cased on the inside with transparent blue. Vasa Murrhina made in Sandwich was seldom reworked. When the glass was reheated to flute the rims or apply handles, it almost always cracked. This problem caused the downfall of the company only eighteen months after its inception. See Chapter 8 in Volume 4. *Courtesy, Sandwich Glass Museum, Sandwich Historical Society*

3083 TREVAISE VASE
4½" H. x 4⅜" Dia. 1907–1908
Trevaise closely resembles the Art Nouveau style of glass made by Louis C. Tiffany. It was produced at the Alton Manufacturing Company in Sandwich, under the direction of a Tiffany employee. Its most notable identifying characteristic is a wafer-shaped piece of glass applied to the center of the base. In most instances, the center of the wafer was dished out and polished, resulting in a *donut*. Some pieces of Tiffany also have a donut, but Tiffany pieces are signed. Volume 4 includes the complete history of the Alton Manufacturing Company in Chapter 4, and the study of Trevaise vases in Chapter 17.

3084 BLOWN MOLDED OPAL FLOWER POT DECORATED WITH BIRD TRANSFER PRINTS

7" H. x 7 ¾" Dia. 1874–1887

This style of flower pot was described as "new shape" in the Boston and Sandwich 1874 catalog. Pots with straight sides could be several years older. A ½" hole in the center of the base was not for drainage, but for attaching to an ornate jardinier stand. The robin shown can be seen on a hanging flower basket pictured on page 57 of the catalog. Today we might not combine orange lines with a lilac floated band, but the overall effect is very attractive.

Courtesy, Sandwich Glass Museum, Sandwich Historical Society

3085 ANOTHER VIEW OF ABOVE FLOWER POT

If you find this hummingbird on another opal piece such as a lamp shade, gas globe, vase, or water bottle and tumbler, it is very likely that the piece is Sandwich.

3086 THIRD VIEW OF ABOVE FLOWER POT

There are three different birds on this same pot. Although all three basic designs were transferred, an artist embellished the designs with shading and detail on the background leaves. The parrot can be seen in the catalog on several styles of vases and a cone shade. Parrots were not native to Cape Cod, but were more common as a household pet than they are today.

3087 BLOWN MOLDED OPAL FLOWER POT DECORATED WITH DOGWOOD AND BEE

7½" H. x 7⅞" Dia. 1880–1887

Decorator Annie Nye began working for the Boston and Sandwich Glass Company in 1880. She was one of the last employees to leave, staying on to complete orders remaining after the factory officially closed. This piece is attributed to her by family descendants. Because there are other family pieces painted in this finely detailed style with a muted background, we concur. Note the veins in the bee's wings and dogwood petals. Again, look for this type of artistry on lamp pedestals and other articles.

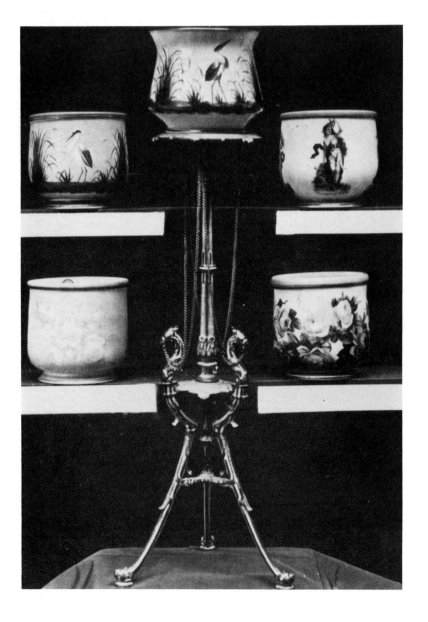

3088 JARDINIER STAND ACCOMPANIED BY BLOWN MOLDED OPAL FLOWER POTS

(a) Jardinier stand 1870–1887

(b) Great Blue Heron "new shape" flower pot 1874–1887

(c) Four decorated straight-sided flower pots 1870–1887

This photo was copied from the original Boston and Sandwich Glass Company 1874 catalog. The company sold this stand, but did not manufacture it. The flower pot was mounted by placing a rubber washer on the threaded fitting of the stand, then positioning the hole in the pot over the fitting. Another washer and a threaded nut, and the pot was firmly in place with a watertight seal. Stones were placed in the decorated glass pot. A plant already planted in a clay pot with a drainage hole was inserted. If the diameter of the clay pot was only slightly less than the inside diameter of the glass pot, excess moisture that drained onto the stones would not evaporate but would find its way back into the soil. This was the advantage of the "new shape" pot. The straight-sided pots that preceded the "new shape" pots by several years could not hold as much water. The catalog identifies the designs only by number. The birds were hand painted, but the figure at the upper right was probably a transfer. *Courtesy, Sandwich Glass Museum, Sandwich Historical Society*

3089 PRESSED STRAIGHT FLOWER TROUGHS
(a) 2" H. x 18" L. x 2" W.
(b) 2" H. x 11½" L. x 2" W.
(c) 2" H. x 8½" L. x 2" W. 1870–1887

Flower troughs were placed end to end on banquet tables, keeping floral arrangements low enough so as not to interfere with conversation. They came in a variety of shapes but were all the same width and pattern of coarse ribs so they could be strung together in any number of configurations. The ones shown in the 1874 catalog are raised on small feet. Some sat flat on the table. They were made in a later mold. Straight troughs varied in length to accommodate the various lengths of tables.

3090 PRESSED BRIDGE FLOWER TROUGH
5½" H. x 11½" L. x 2" W. 1870–1887

Bridges had several uses. They were placed every several feet in the "run" with flowers in the end compartments. Mints or bonbons in the center compartment and stick candy or candy canes fanned out from the vertical compartments, delighting both adults and children. They were also used to bridge the gap between two tables that were not the same height.

3091 PRESSED GONDOLA
5" H. x 11¾" L. x 2" W. 1870–1887

The gondola is designed like the bridge. Four partitions divide it into five chambers. It was not used for flowers, but was positioned in the "run" at right angles. "Red hots" were placed in the end sections where they could be easily scooped out. The candy sticks and treats in the other compartments could only be eaten with permission from Mother, who could reach over the ends without rocking the gondola.

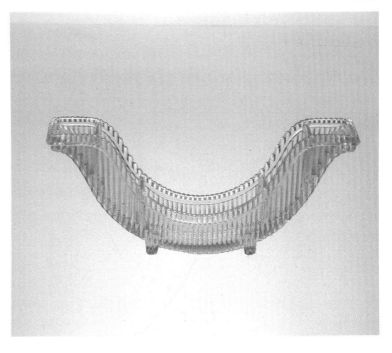

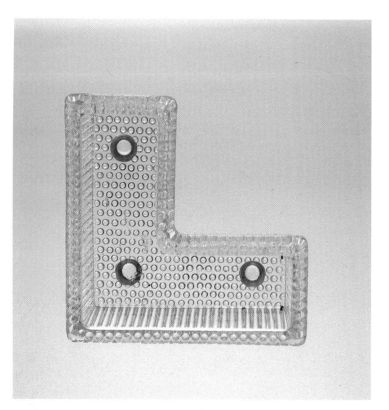

3092 PRESSED ANGLE FLOWER TROUGH
2" H. x 4¾" L. x 4¾" W. 1870-1887

Train and boat excursions to political rallies and camp meetings were a large part of Nineteenth Century social life. As many as one thousand people would attend a celebration or jubilee. An elderly lady recalling a strawberry festival in an enormous barn told about red clover and purple vetch being arranged in troughs. For a harvest supper in the Fall, bittersweet and bursting milkweed pods were used. The angle trough units were most commonly used when a row of tables made a 90 degree turn. Four units could make a square in the center of a square table or a rectangle when combined with straight units.

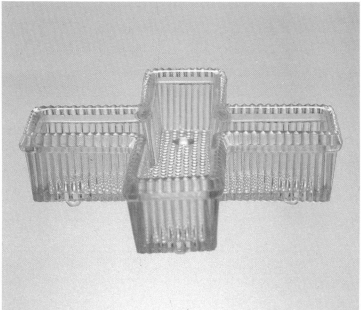

3093 PRESSED CROSS FLOWER TROUGH
2" H. x 7" L. x 7" W. 1870-1887

We have known of this piece being combined with a straight unit to make a cross at a church function. Flower troughs meant to be combined were made in clear glass. Fresh flowers were used in Spring and Summer. For a large gathering, it was difficult to use fresh flowers because the shallow containers did not hold enough water and the flowers wilted if they were arranged the day before.

3094 PRESSED TRIANGLE FLOWER TROUGH
2" H.; 5" L. on short sides; 6½" L. on long side
1870-1887

Triangles were used to fill in when the centerpieces required it. This one has three feet. It can also be found with a flat base, like the other units. Note the dug fragment. It is the 90 degree corner and shows the same defect as the complete piece. Unlike the beaded rims of the other pieces, the corners of the triangle are smooth. The hot glass did not flow readily into the corners, especially the 45 degree ones. A later change in mold design corrected the problem.

3095 PRESSED QUARTER CIRCLE FLOWER TROUGHS
To make a 14" Dia. circle 1870–1887

Quarter circles and half circles were arranged around a centerpiece, which might be a salver or an elaborate epergne if the social function was in a home or hotel. Epergnes held fruit and nuts and even more flowers. Salvers are called *cake plates* today, but in Victorian times several arranged vertically held dessert jellies and sweets. It has been suggested to us that the Victorian table must have resembled a junk yard.

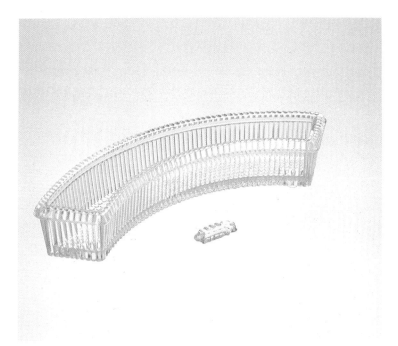

3096 PRESSED HALF CIRCLE FLOWER TROUGHS
To make a 12" Dia. circle 1870–1887

Several sizes of half circles were marketed to make different diameter full circles. A smaller size in our collection makes a 9½" circle. Metal flower holders that could be cut to any length were inserted as shown here.

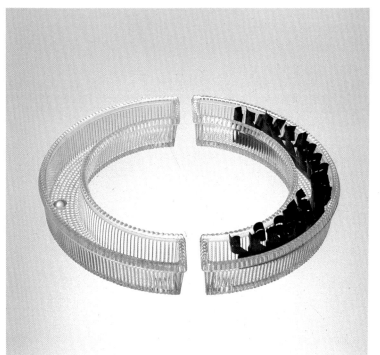

3097 METAL FLOWER HOLDER FOR TROUGHS
Two types of flower holders were made to be used in flower troughs. The two shown here were made by coating a sheet of copper with hot lead. The lead adhered to the copper, giving it weight. The copper sheet was cut into strips ½" wide. The strips were twisted into stem holders. Later inserts were made of wire springs.

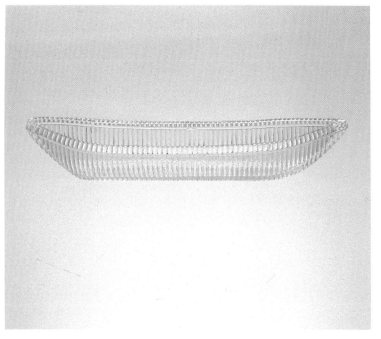

3098 PRESSED BOAT DISH

2" H. x 12" L. x 2" W. 1870–1887

The boat was sold as an accessory to the troughs but was not used in the "run". It was used as a dish for sweets elsewhere on the table. For a small gathering, there is no reason why it could not have doubled as a relish dish. Each unit was marketed and priced individually. The customer made his selection to fit his needs.

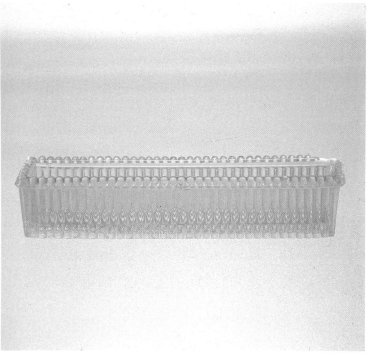

3099 PRESSED FIERY OPALESCENT STRAIGHT FLOWER TROUGH

2" H. x 9" L. x 2" W. 1870–1887

The troughs meant to be purchased in bulk were made from clear glass. Occasionally a unit was selected to be made in color to be used singly. This piece has an underfilled corner. Underfill can be found anywhere around the rims of troughs because, even in color, this was an inexpensive item and quality control was not a consideration. If it was used in an office and broken, who cared? The underfill would be hidden by the floral arrangement. Underfill is caused by not pressing enough glass into the mold.

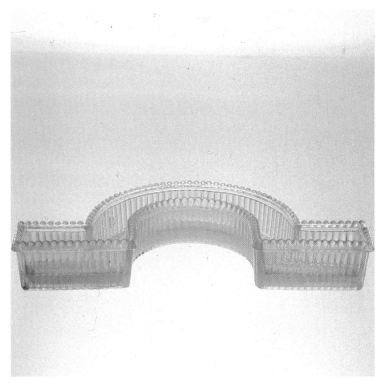

3100 PRESSED FIERY OPALESCENT HALF CIRCLE WITH EXTENSIONS FLOWER TROUGH

2" H. x 12" L. x 5¼" W. 1870–1887

There are no partitions between the half circle and the two extensions. One long metal insert could be easily bent to follow the shape of the unit. We have one documented use of this shape trough. Two units were placed back to back across the top of a roll top desk in a business establishment. An inkwell was in each half-circle for the use of anyone who walked up to the desk to sign papers for the clerk who was sitting behind the desk. The troughs, filled with flowers, held the inkwell in place.

COLOGNES

1840–1887

Bottles can be divided generally into three categories. First are the traditional commercial types such as flasks, wines, medicine, and extract bottles. Although records do show that the Board of Directors of the Boston and Sandwich Glass Company authorized the making of green bottle glass, this was only during a period of severe depression. The usual commercial bottles did not represent a large part of the company's production, nor did they at the Cape Cod Glass Works. These orders were best filled by glass houses specializing in bottles, utilizing a less expensive glass made from an inferior grade of sand. The second category covers highly specialized commercial bottles that were designed for a specific purpose, either by the glass companies or by wholesale houses that sent their private bottle molds to the glass factory. After receiving the empty bottles from the manufacturer, the wholesale houses filled them with their own product, such as smelling salts or perfume. These specialized commercial bottles were made in relatively large quantities at Sandwich, and will be treated in another chapter. In the third category are the decorative bottles that contained cologne, which was perfume diluted with alcohol. Cologne bottles were made from high quality glass that required the special talents of individual workmen. Although an order for colognes would be occasionally sent out to a retailer to be labeled and filled with his product, most were sold through glass company showrooms or outlying agencies directly to the retail customer, to be used on bureaus and dressing tables.

The colognes shown here represent only a small fraction of Sandwich's output. The quantity of stoppers of elegant form and color that were dug at the Boston and Sandwich Glass Company site strengthens the belief that production of cologne bottles was extensive. Living in today's society, it is difficult for us to realize that, in the Nineteenth Century, cologne was a most practical necessity. People did not have the convenience of hot and cold running water for bathing. Nor did they have washers and dryers to automatically launder their clothing. Personal hygiene was a constant problem, intensified by the heat of a summer day and made unbearable by the heavy woolen cloth-

ing of winter. The use of cologne was as common as today's use of deodorants. In addition to its use at home, cologne was regularly carried by women in their purses for that "pause that refreshes". The small purse-size bottles were filled with a tiny funnel.

Information on the earliest cologne bottles is scanty. They are listed late in 1825 in Sandwich Glass Manufactory records, but with no description other than that some had mushroom stoppers. All of the colognes designed for milady's dressing table which will be discussed in this chapter were manufactured from approximately 1840. They all have glass stoppers that match the bottle in form and color. The plug of the stopper and/or the throat (the inside of the neck) of the cologne were machined to create a perfect fit, to prevent evaporation of the contents. After a stopper was fitted to a bottle, it very often was numbered. The same number was inscribed on the bottle, either in the neck, lip, or base. All of the colognes that can positively be attributed to Sandwich are inscribed with Arabic numerals. There are a number of Overlay colognes with Roman numerals, but these are closely identified with Nineteenth Century French Overlay pieces shown in Yolande Amic's *L'Opaline Francaise au XIXe Siecle*, published in Paris in 1952.

Occasionally a cologne is found with a stopper that appears to be its mate, but does not seat snugly. It may wobble slightly, or goes either too deeply or not deeply enough into the throat. If it is numbered and the numbers match, we must be satisfied that the piece is correct and that not enough care had gone into its fitting. If the number of the stopper does not match the number on the cologne, it is very possible that the cologne was one of a pair or a set, and the stoppers were switched. If you are buying one of a pair, and the seller has both, check the stoppers of each to make sure that each stopper is in the correct bottle. *Half the value of a cologne is in its stopper*. Even an inexpensive clear glass cologne is substantially decreased in value if its stopper is not original. (Because stoppers are an important means of identifying Sandwich glass, we have devoted an entire chapter to the more than eight thousand stoppers dug from the site of the Boston and Sandwich Glass Company.) If a cologne stopper can be positively identified as Sandwich, and appears to fit properly into a bottle that matches in color and form, it is possible that the entire unit can be attributed to Sandwich.

Many Sandwich colognes can readily be identified by associating their patterns and designs with other known Sandwich articles. For example, several colognes are identical in pattern to lamp fonts, such as Heart and Waisted Loop. Oval Hobnail pattern was made in colognes, puff boxes, newel post finials and vases. Designs that were copper wheel engraved on tableware during the Late Blown Period can also be found on Sandwich colognes.

There are almost one hundred Overshot, copper wheel engraved, and cut glass colognes pictured in the 1874 Boston and Sandwich Glass Company catalog. They are identified as colognes in the price list to the catalog, preserved at the Sandwich Glass Museum. Most of them are on pages 3, 9, and 10 of the catalog. There are also several plain colognes in the catalog which were used as *blanks* for Threaded Glass colognes after 1880.

As we studied Sandwich colognes, we were able to verify a fact that had been established by Ruth Webb Lee in 1939: no octagonal colognes can be attributed to Sandwich. Sandwich bottles are hexagonal, round, square, or square with chamferred corners. An occasional *cut* octagonal cologne may be found, but a *round* bottle was used for a blank.

It is essential that Sandwich glass attribution be based upon *at least* two methods of identification (described below) for an important reason: the Boston and Sandwich Glass Company, like other glass manufacturers in this country, routinely copied patterns when they saw something they liked. It was a common industry practice.

That is why many of the patterns we know for certain were made in Sandwich also appear in French catalogs of the 1840's, such as those of Cristalleries de Baccarat and Cristalleries de Saint Louis.

As early as 1927, Rhea Mansfield Knittle pointed out in her book *Early American Glass* that some patterns made in Sandwich could not be distinguished from those turned out by Launay & Cie of France.

The records show, furthermore, that the Boston and Sandwich Glass Company sent representatives several times to Europe to study methods of glassmaking. George Franklin Lapham went to study etching, and, in 1869, Superintendent George Lafayette Fessenden went to actually *acquire* patent rights for foreign molds and patterns.

So, when a piece of glass is found illustrated in an original factory catalog, it is a mistake, *on that basis alone*, to attribute that piece exclusively to that factory.

Throughout our research and writing, therefore, we have constantly attributed Sandwich glass only with the security that comes from the use of two or more of the following methods of identification:

- Fragments of bottles dug at factory sites.
- Whole stoppers dug at factory sites.
- Catalogs printed at the time of production.
- Company invoices, records, and other documents.
- Family heirlooms belonging to descendants of glassworkers, with accompanying documentation.
- Newspaper advertisements and articles written at the time of production.

In 1925, Bangs Burgess wrote an article telling about going into the Boston and Sandwich Glass Company factory. Miss Burgess was the niece of glassworker Thomas Heffernan, who had taken her on a tour of the factory when she was a child. Her father and grandfather had also worked in the factory, so she was well versed in the art of glassmaking.

> There was one lovely old man whom I remember as a child called Mr. Bonique, who was the gaffer of the castor place shop, so-called. What he really did was made odds and ends from patterns. *I once saw him copying a perfumery bottle*, that had a broken stopper, of a then celebrated actress. Her order was that they were to drill a hole in the old bottle and get the perfumery out without waste.

The important statement here was the fact that he took the time to copy the bottle. We would assume that if he was copying the design of the bottle, it was not a Sandwich bottle, but soon would be. So copying each other's product whenever the opportunity presented itself was an everyday occurrence at a glass factory.

THESE SIMPLE HINTS WILL HELP YOU IDENTIFY SANDWICH COLOGNES.

Colognes have glass stoppers.

Study the chapter on stoppers. Stopper identification is a useful tool.

Check to determine if the attributed stopper is original to the cologne.

If a number is inscribed on the cologne, the same number should be inscribed on the stopper.

Colognes with Roman numerals cut into them are not Sandwich.

Study the Boston and Sandwich Glass Company 1874 catalog.

Identify by association. Study other articles of identical design and pattern, such as lamp fonts, finials, salts, and vases.

3101 BLOWN MOLDED RING AND STAR (STAR AND PUNTY) COLOGNES

(a) Small neck 5⅛" H. without stopper
(b) Large neck 5¼" H. without stopper 1841–1870

We have deliberately removed the stoppers so that you can study the neck of each cologne. The neck on the right bottle is thicker and higher. All of these pieces were worked to some extent by hand, which accounts for the variation in dimensions. Even though the necks vary, the colognes are considered a pair. We give you exact measurements of the piece we are working with, but the student of glass who attributes a piece to a certain company based on dimensions alone is usually wrong. Be careful when handling stoppers not to mix them up. They are individually machined to fit each bottle and are so numbered. Mixed stoppers downgrade a cologne's value. The stopper shown here does not have an air pocket because it was pressed in a stopper wheel mold.

3102 BLOWN MOLDED RING AND STAR (STAR AND PUNTY) COLOGNE

6¾" H. x 2¾" Dia. 1840–1870

This pattern was very popular, and is often seen in this color. The same pattern was also used to make lamp fonts, pitchers, and spoon holders. This cologne is very heavy because the walls are exceptionally thick. A pontil rod was used on all pieces made in this pattern while they were being reworked into various configurations, so a polished pontil mark is on the base of the cologne. The cologne and its stopper both have the same number inscribed. Note the stopper. It has a large air pocket that is clearly visible and was unquestionably blown into a stopper mold.

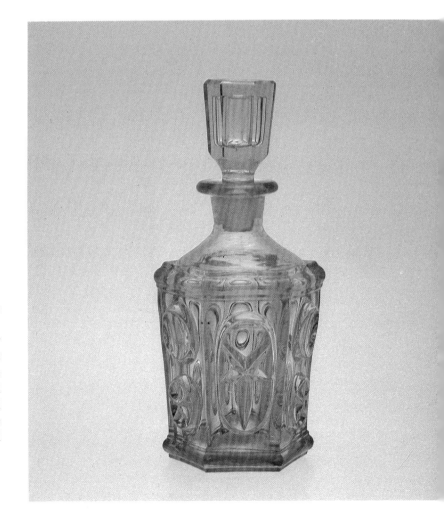

3103 BLOWN MOLDED LYRE (HARP) COLOGNE

6⅛" H. x 3⅛" Dia. 1840–1870

This pattern is sometimes called Harp, as it was in the 1859–1860 catalog of McKee and Brothers from Pittsburgh, Pennsylvania. This piece, however, was made in Sandwich. The overall shape of this cologne is the same as Star and Punty in photo 3101. Only the design in the panels changes. There are six lyres (harps), one in each panel. The mold used to make this cologne was badly worn. The base of the instruments and the strings are not well defined. This does not detract from the value of the piece. The flat, square stopper has chamferred corners. It is a pressed stopper, and is numbered to match the cologne. *Courtesy, Sandwich Glass Museum, Sandwich Historical Society*

3104 BLOWN MOLDED HEART COLOGNE

7⅛" H. x 3¾" Dia. 1840–1860

In order to truly appreciate the design of this pressed cologne, turn the picture upside down. Only then will you realize that it was made from the mold for the font of the Heart lamp. Used as a cologne, the hearts are upside down. The base of the cologne is where the dome on the top of the font would be. What would have been the extension underneath the font has been formed into the neck of the cologne. A pressed, cut stopper was inserted. The shape of the stopper is not critical to this piece. It can be found with other stoppers, but the stopper and bottle should be inscribed with the same number.

3105 BLOWN MOLDED BABY THUMBPRINT COLOGNE

7" H. x 3" Dia. 1840–1860

This cologne is covered with round thumbprints on the *outside* of the bottle. If the outside surface is smooth, and the pattern shows through from the inside, the piece would not be Sandwich. No fragments have ever been found at the factory site with a surface pattern that came in contact with its contents, such as the inside of a pitcher or vase, or the upper surface of a plate. The stopper and the bottles are inscribed with the same number. The bottle and the stopper tip slightly off center, the result of overheating in the annealing oven (leer). This does not detract from its value. Small imperfections are characteristic of antique glass, and are useful identification marks when describing your glass on the inventory pages of this book.

3106 BLOWN MOLDED LOOP (LEAF) COLOGNE

6½" H. x 3" Dia. 1840–1860

The pattern known as Loop today was called Leaf by the glass companies that made it. This includes the Boston and Sandwich Glass Company, Cape Cod Glass Company, and McKee and Brothers from Pittsburgh, Pennsylvania. This cologne was made in Sandwich, using the mold for a lamp font. The glass that would have formed the knop under the lamp font was reshaped to become the foot of the bottle. The glass that would have been the dome of the font was drawn to make the neck. Note how light the color is in the part of the glass that was drawn. It is so thin that little pigment is left, making the glass look almost clear. The stopper and bottle have matching numbers.

3107 BLOWN MOLDED WASTED LOOP COLOGNE WITH FLOWER STOPPER

5" H. x 2½" Dia. 1840–1870

This cologne holds two ounces of liquid. A puff box was made to match. The flower stopper appears just as it came out of the mold. Sometimes the petals were reworked to flare out or to close into a bud. We point this out to impress on you why it is important to study how glass articles were constructed. Note also that Sandwich colognes have six, not eight, sides. This flower stopper and bottle was also produced by Cristalleries de Baccarat in France, and can be seen in the Launay Hautin & Compagnie catalogs. We have not seen a reworked stopper on the French pieces that we have examined.

3108 BLOWN MOLDED ELONGATED LOOP COLOGNES

7" H. x 3" Dia. 1840–1870

The Boston and Sandwich Glass Company very often used a flower motif. The Petal candle socket, the Easter Lily towel holder, and the Tulip vase are several examples. To fully enjoy the floral effect of this cologne, turn the photo upside down. The graceful flow of the design becomes apparent. Each of the six panels has an elongated loop. The panel is carried to the lip. The petal protrusions at the base stand out ¾" from the body. The stopper, normally the same width as the lip, was made larger to repeat the petal design. This piece is often gilded, as on the stopper fragment.

3109 BLOWN MOLDED ELONGATED LOOP COLOGNE
6½" H. x 3" Dia. 1840–1870

The spike on the stopper varies in height up to ½", depending on the mold. On some pieces, the elongated loops have bars across their centers. Keep in mind that color in no way determines where a piece was manufactured. This cologne is "depression green", and was passed over by many experienced collectors because of its color. This bottle and stopper was also made by Cristalleries de Baccarat in France. The bottle with a different stopper is illustrated in an 1868 catalog from the New England Glass Company. A similar bottle was reproduced by perfume houses in 1983. The Sandwich and Baccarat colognes have polished pontil marks. The New England Glass Company cologne and the reproduction do not.

3110 BLOWN MOLDED OVAL PANELLED FRAMES COLOGNES WITH LILY STOPPER
(a) Amber with gilding and cut neck 6¾" H. x 3¼" Dia. 1845–1870
(b) Green canary 7" H. x 3¼" Dia. 1840–1870

This cologne is often attributed to France because a similar one was made by Cristalleries de Baccarat in the 1840's. Note the reinforcing ring half way down the neck. This ring is not on the Baccarat piece, as shown in the illustration. Many fragments of the bottle and stopper were dug at the Boston and Sandwich Glass Company site, and descendants of Sandwich glassworkers have this cologne in their family collections. No gilding was done at Sandwich prior to the arrival of gilder William Smith by 1845. This accounts for the difference in the dating of the two Sandwich colognes in the photo. The term *vaseline* was not used in the 1800's. Yellow with a green tinge was called *green canary*.

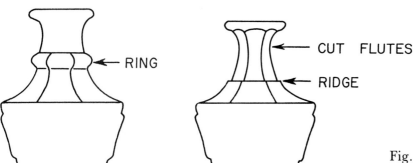

Fig. 8 The Sandwich cologne has a reinforcing ring around a plain neck. The neck of the Baccarat cologne is cut into six flutes beginning at the lip and terminating abruptly in a horizontal line that makes a slight ridge above the shoulder. Both colognes have a Lily stopper.

William Smith, first gilder at the Boston and Sandwich Glass Company, arrived in Boston from England on January 7, 1844. He was the father of the Smith Brothers, who were known for decorating on opal glass. *Courtesy, Sandwich Glass Museum, Sandwich Historical Society*

3111 BLOWN MOLDED COLOGNE
5½" H. x 2½" Dia. 1840–1870
Clear fragments of this cologne and this stopper have been found at the Boston and Sandwich Glass Company site in large quantities, but the cologne shown here is the only one we have seen in color. The stopper is machined to fit unusually tight. When stoppers fit this tightly, care should be taken to move them periodically to prevent them from sealing. Expect this cologne to be heavy for its size, because the thickness of the walls limits its contents to less than one ounce. Although blown, the stopper matches the drawing in Hiram Dillaway's patent number 2226 for a pressed stopper wheel, dated August 21, 1841, which can be seen in the stoppers chapter in this book.

3112 BLOWN MOLDED COLOGNE
5½" H. 1840–1870
A clear glass cologne identical to the one shown here was dug in almost perfect condition at the site of the Boston and Sandwich Glass Company. It is so heavy that it holds very little. There are six large convex circles around the body, with six almond-shaped ovals above. The stopper has an air trap in its center, indicating that it was blown into a mold.

3113 BLOWN MOLDED PANELLED DIAMOND POINT COLOGNE

5⅝" H. x 3¾" Dia. 1840–1860

Decorative bottles with alternating panels were very popular during this period, and were produced by most glass manufacturers. The Sandwich cologne can accurately be identified only by matching it with fragments from the factory site. Alternating rows of six and seven full diamonds in each panel are common in the Sandwich diggings. The stopper and the three rings on the shoulder of this cologne have also been found at the site. The soft green color is found in the fragments, although not in the form of a cologne. The slight protrusion of the raised base indicates there may have been an underplate similar to 3121.

3114 BLOWN MOLDED COLOGNE WITH FLOWER STOPPER

7¼" H. x 2¾" Dia. 1850–1870

This is an example of a cologne with a different color stopper which is original to the bottle. Using different colored stoppers was an accepted procedure at the time of manufacture. The number on the stopper matches the number on the bottle. Once again, do not determine origin by color. This cologne in brassy green would be thought by many to be French, but it was produced at the Boston and Sandwich Glass Company. *Courtesy, Sandwich Glass Museum, Sandwich Historical Society*

3115 BLOWN MOLDED ROSETTE COLOGNE

7½" H. x 3⅛" Dia. 1845–1870

This cologne is made up of five-petaled rosettes placed in nine rows around the body. Some areas have large flat spaces between the rosettes. The top row near the shoulder shows some flattening of the petals, caused by reheating the bottle to form the neck. A very deeply polished pontil mark is on the base, and there is gilding on the shoulder, neck, and base. The flower stopper was married to the bottle at a later date. There is a number inscribed on the base of the cologne, but no number on the stopper, which looks top-heavy. *Courtesy, Sandwich Glass Museum, Sandwich Historical Society*

3116 BLOWN MOLDED ROSETTE COLOGNE WITH UMBRELLA STOPPER

7¾" H. x 3¼" Dia. 1840–1870

This cologne is the same as the previous one, but was not gilded. The raised foot on both bottles was blown as part of the original piece. By looking down into the bottle, a penetration into the foot can be seen. The pressed umbrella stopper has eight segments, and a three-ringed knop in the center of the shank. The stopper was also produced by Cristalleries de Saint Louis in France. *Courtesy, Sandwich Glass Museum, Sandwich Historical Society*

3117 BLOWN MOLDED ROSETTE COLOGNE
4⅜" H. x 2⅛" Dia. 1840–1870
The shape of this cologne lends itself to nine rows of evenly-spaced five-petaled rosettes. The rosettes are small on the shoulder and near the base, and larger in the center. The six-lobed stopper is original and can be found on many other colognes made in Sandwich. *Courtesy, Sandwich Glass Museum, Sandwich Historical Society*

3118 BLOWN MOLDED OVAL HOBNAIL COLOGNES
(a) Rings on shoulder, six-lobed stopper
    5½" H. x 2½" Dia.
(b) No rings on shoulder, Hobnail stopper
    4½" H. x 1⅞" Dia. 1840–1870
This hobnail pattern is unique because it does not imitate the round flattened hobnail made by other manufacturers. Therefore, we have added the word *Oval* in its description. Colognes with this pattern were made in several sizes. A puff box (powder jar) was made to match, and can be seen in the chapter on covered containers. A pair of colognes and a puff box were sometimes sold as a three piece toilet set. The stopper on cologne A is identical to the one on the previous Rosette cologne. The stopper on cologne B has a hobnail pattern. This cologne is a family heirloom from the descendants of head gaffer Theodore Kern.

3119 BLOWN MOLDED OVAL HOBNAIL COLOGNE

5" H. x 2½" Dia. 1845–1870

The French influence can be seen in Sandwich glass in both color and pattern. Quantities of fragments dug at the Boston and Sandwich Glass Company site show the upper rows of hobnails and the ring above them. The gilding around the base indicates that the cologne did not have an underplate. The stopper has been dug in a variety of colors and was used on other colognes as well. *Courtesy, Sandwich Glass Museum, Sandwich Historical Society*

3120 BLOWN MOLDED OVAL HOBNAIL COLOGNE WITH FLOWER STOPPER

6½" H. x 3" Dia. 1845–1870

The flower stopper is a standard type used on many pieces produced by the Boston and Sandwich Glass Company. The mixed color combination is correct because the stopper fits perfectly and is numbered to match the number on the cologne. The tips of the hobnails are gilded, and a band of gilding can be seen surrounding the base. The Oval Hobnail pattern was used on other pieces as well, including lamp fonts. This cologne is closely related in design to several of the vases shown in this book, and to the finial shown later.

3121 OVAL HOBNAIL

(a) Blown molded cologne with pressed flower stopper
   8" H. x 4" Dia.
(b) Pressed underplate 1" H. x 5" Dia.
(c) Blown molded finial for newel posts and curtain rods 5¾" H. x 2¾" Dia. 1840–1870

The Boston and Sandwich Glass Company frequently used the same pattern to make several different items. It is important, therefore, to become familiar with the other items. The cologne and the underplate have polished pontil marks, indicating that they were blown into the mold. The cologne was reworked in the neck, throat, and expanded lip. The clambroth underplate and stoppers are fragments dug at the site of the factory and match the blue pieces perfectly.

3122 BLOWN MOLDED SNAKE ENTWINED COLOGNE
6" H. x 2¾" Dia. 1841–1860
Once again we see the simple lines of Sandwich molds. This smoky clambroth cologne was blown into a mold, like the one in the next photo. The snake was applied with its head at the bottom. The Dillaway stopper, matching in color and fitting perfectly, completes the piece. The shape of the stopper is illustrated in Hiram Dillaway's patent for making many pressed stoppers simultaneously. His patent can be seen in Chapter 6 about stoppers in this book. Keep in mind that foreign glass companies shipped great quantities of colognes with serpents wrapped around them into this country. It is difficult to identify Sandwich bottles of this style without family connections.

3123 BLOWN MOLDED RING-NECKED COLOGNE
3½" H. x 2" Dia. 1850–1860
This cologne combines a blown bottle with a pressed stopper, both opaque white. At one time, each was gilded, but most of the gilding has worn away. A translucent blue ring encircles the piece near the shoulder. Generally, the simple lines of bottles such as this make attribution to a specific glass house difficult. We can attribute this cologne to Sandwich, however, because the stopper has been found in the diggings, and several necks with both blue and green rings have been found in the area of the dump believed to have been used in 1850. The stopper is numbered to match the number on the bottle.

3124 BLOWN MOLDED COVERED BASKET COLOGNE
4⅞" H. x 2½" Dia. 1850–1870

Although this cologne was molded in one piece, it was designed to look like two pieces. Note the double line around the bottle, representing the rims of the basket and its cover. A plain neck was added to the basket cover. The stopper takes its ribbed pattern from the basket cover. Gilded lines surround the neck of the cologne and the shoulder of the stopper, which is inscribed with a number that matches the number on the cologne. This is one of the few examples of figural glass made in Sandwich. Several types of baskets were made, all from glass of excellent quality and all with patterns of wicker basket weave. The difference between the Sandwich weave and the weave made at Compagnie des Cristalleries de Baccarat, located in Baccarat, France, is shown in the illustration below. Both patterns were made during the same period out of exceptionally beautiful glass. Midwest and French companies later used Sandwich's pattern on figural match or toothpick holders of lesser quality. *Courtesy, Sandwich Glass Museum, Sandwich Historical Society*

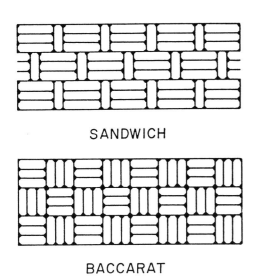

SANDWICH

BACCARAT

Fig. 9 The Sandwich basket pattern is a wicker weave composed of three pliable horizontal rods woven over and under widely spaced, single, rigid vertical rods. The Baccarat weave of three horizontal rods woven under and over three closely spaced vertical rods gives the effect of a splint basket.

3125 BLOWN MOLDED RIBBED COLOGNE
5" H. x 2½" Dia. 1850–1870

The similarities between this cologne and the previous one can easily be seen. The ribs, also used on the Boston and Sandwich Glass Company's Onion lamp, run up the side, over the shoulder, and stop at the neck. The plain neck sits atop the bottle like an afterthought, in the same manner as 3124. The stopper repeats the design of the cologne. It is the same stopper as the previous one, and in size is interchangeable. But it was machined to fit this cologne and is numbered to match it.

3126 BLOWN MOLDED ARTICHOKE COLOGNE
7" H. 1845–1860

This is one of Sandwich's most striking cologne patterns. Note the rib on each artichoke scale, both on the cologne and stopper. Although this shade of green is extremely rare, it is the only color in which this cologne has been found. The gilding is well preserved on both units. Do not let a lack of gilding discourage your purchase of this bottle. Fragments dug at the factory site show no gilding. The stopper is numbered, and the matching number is inscribed on the polished pontil mark. A similar cologne was made by Cristalleries de Baccarat. The French bottle has a plain rim and the neck is fluted. Note the differences in the illustration.

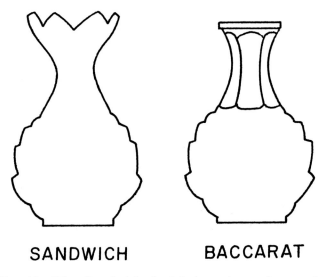

SANDWICH   BACCARAT

Fig. 10 The Sandwich Artichoke cologne has a plain neck and a petaled rim. The Baccarat cologne has a fluted neck and a plain rim.

3127 CUT PRISM AND SHARP DIAMOND COLOGNE WITH SIGNED STOPPER
9½" H. x 3½" Dia. 1841

George Franklin Lapham joined the Boston and Sandwich Glass Company in 1836, when he was fourteen years old. Five years later, with his apprenticeship completed, he had become a skilled glass cutter at the age of nineteen. This cut glass cologne is one of many exquisite Sandwich pieces from the Lapham family collection. The bottle was cut with panels, and the lower part was cut into a diamond motif. The stopper was cut to match the panels in the neck. Note the ring around the neck, a characteristic of Sandwich colognes.

3128 SIGNED STOPPER FROM ABOVE COLOGNE

The bottom of the stopper plug is inscribed "Oct 1841 F. Lapham", the signature of George Franklin Lapham, called Frank. The fact that he signed as many pieces as he did for his private collection is evidence of the pride he had in his work.

George Franklin Lapham, glass cutter.

3129 CUT SHARP DIAMOND COLOGNE

3½" H. x 3¾" Dia. 1840–1860

This is an example of a cologne that was originally identified by its stopper. Several such stoppers were dug at the site of the Boston and Sandwich Glass Company, but we did not know at the time what type of bottle the stopper was designed to go with. The stopper blank was shaped like a mushroom. Large diamonds were cut into it, which were then crudely crosshatched. The diamond design shown on the cologne is not repeated on the stopper. This was a common practice at Sandwich. The stopper is numbered to match the cologne. The cut Sharp Diamond design is sharp to the touch and is very well preserved. Cut prisms radiate from a polished pontil mark on the base to the Sharp Diamond design.

3130 CUT SHARP DIAMOND GLOBE COLOGNE

7½" H. x 4¾" Dia. without stopper 1870–1887

Globe colognes were made in many sizes and in several cut designs. There is a Fine Diamond design, which has a small diamond, and the Octagon Diamond design seen in photo 3154. The neck is paneled and there are concentric circles on the shoulder. There should be a faceted stopper with a rather long shank. Other glass companies *pressed* reproductions in the same pattern. They are often sold as Sandwich, but only the *cut* colognes have been authenticated as Sandwich. The pressed reproductions have pressed stoppers with a matching diamond pattern. The Boston and Sandwich Glass Company made matching puff boxes. The finial on the puff box cover is cut into facets to match the cologne stopper. *Courtesy, Sandwich Glass Museum, Sandwich Historical Society*

3131 CUT SHARP DIAMOND COLOGNE
5¾" H. x 2½" Dia. 1870–1887

A study of the 1874 catalog reveals that, by 1870, cut designs with several elements had given way to geometric designs repeated over the whole body. The blanks were made in as many as eight sizes, both round and square. Mass produced lapidary stoppers were fitted to each bottle rather than custom made stoppers. This saved on production costs, because if a stopper was chipped during fitting, a new one did not have to be cut with a matching design. The Sharp Diamond design was cut in horizontal rows as shown here and, more often, in diagonal rows as shown in the catalog. The steps on the shoulder were made by cutting concentric rings around the bottle. Be aware that the designs shown on colognes in the Boston and Sandwich Glass Company catalog are *cut* designs.

3132 CUT BLOCK DIAMOND COLOGNE
7⅜" H.; 2½" square at base 1870–1887

At one point, this piece was a square bottle blank. The lines to be cut were drawn on the surface, and the design was then cut and polished. This blank can be seen in the Boston and Sandwich Glass Company 1874 catalog. The Block Diamond design can be seen on a pickle jar in the same catalog. In the 1870's, straight-forward geometric designs were cut over the entire body of a piece. Square puff boxes were made to match the colognes. The puff boxes are very seldom found today. *Courtesy, Sandwich Glass Museum, Sandwich Historical Society*

3133 CUT BLOCK DIAMOND WITH STAR COLOGNE
8¼" H.; 2¾" square at base 1870–1887

This cologne has the simple squares of the Block Diamond design with an eight-pointed star cut and polished in each block. Note the steps made by cutting into the shoulder of the bottle. If this bottle blank had been round, the cutting on the shoulder would appear to be concentric rings. This piece has nine horizontal rows of blocks and six vertical rows on each side. When this design is cut into a smaller blank, each block would be about the same size as on this piece, but there would be fewer rows. The whole bottle has a sameness of design which was characteristic of cut glass designs in the 1870's and 1880's. *Courtesy, Sandwich Glass Museum, Sandwich Historical Society*

3134 CUT QUATREFOIL AND HONEYCOMB COLOGNE

5½" H. x 2¼" Dia. 1860–1880

This cologne is identifiable as Sandwich because of the five quatrefoils cut into the sidewalls, a design which is frequently found on Sandwich Overlay lamp fonts. Three rows of honeycomb are cut into the lower third of the bottle, extending to the base. The lapidary stopper is inscribed with a number that matches the number inscribed on the cologne. The blank for this cologne can be found on page 10 of the Boston and Sandwich Glass Company catalog.

3135 CUT OVERLAY COLOGNE

6¼" H. x 3⅛" Dia. 1845–1860

Overlay is glass cased on the outside with a different color, which is then cut back to reveal the glass beneath. A piece that was cased with one layer of glass was called *plated*, and a piece with two layers of outside casing was called *double plated*. Do not look for perfection in Sandwich Overlay. For example, this cologne was cased with blue glass, then sent to the cutting shop, where the design was marked. Careless cutting created great irregularities in the design. The spacing between the circles (punties) varies, and the blue lines vary in thickness. The stopper was blown and cased with a blue overlay. Its hollow core can be seen in the photo. *On loan to Sandwich Glass Museum, Sandwich Historical Society from the Hollander Family Collection*

3136 CUT OVERLAY COLOGNE

6¼" H. x 3⅜" Dia. 1845–1860

One of the most gratifying experiences of digging at Sandwich for fragments was finding fragments to a piece we already had and knowing they will match. Quantities of fragments matching this cologne were found in red, blue, and green. The red fragment shown here matches the neck of the bottle. The stopper matches the bottle in form, design, and color. It is inscribed with the same number that is on the bottle. In 1844, the Boston and Sandwich Glass Company erected a small furnace for the manufacture of colored glass to be used in plated ware. The earliest Overlay pieces are crude. It took some time to perfect the technique. Pieces of the outer layer would flake during annealing.

3137 CUT OVERLAY PUNTY COLOGNE
8" H. x 2½" Dia. 1845–1865

During thirty years of digging at the site of the Boston and Sandwich Glass Company, we unearthed only a very few perfect pieces. This cologne is by far the greatest find. It was five feet under the ground, near the factory end of the horse railroad. It took five weeks to free the stopper from the bottle, both of which are inscribed with the same number. Other than a slight sickness inside the bottle, it remains today in mint condition. The design is a simple one of circular cutouts called *punties*. The blue overlay is very thick. A polished pontil mark is on the base. The reinforcing ring around the neck is found on many Sandwich colognes.

3138 CUT OVERLAY COLOGNE
5½" H. x 3¼" Dia. 1848–1860

In the late 1840's and early 1850's the quality of the glass company's products improved. Here is an outstanding example of that excellence. In addition to the cut panels on the side, this cologne has a rayed star on the base. This bottle can also be found with a clear cut faceted stopper. Watch for a wide protruding lip that shows the predominant color, in this instance, blue. Often the lip becomes nicked and is then cut down, taking away the colored outer layer. If the lip is gone, you may be sure that you are looking at a badly damaged piece. Repairing glass does *not* add to its value. In the eyes of the advanced collector, it is a damaged piece.

3139 CUT OVERLAY COLOGNE
5½" H. to flattened finial; 2¾" Dia. 1850–1870

This cologne demonstrates the greater skills of Sandwich workers in later years. This bottle is an outstanding example of aesthetic sensibility in combining color and form. The lip of this cologne has been turned up and scalloped, giving the piece a flower effect. The neck has been cut into panels to show the plug of the stopper. A teardrop blown into the plug is centered in the neck panels. Unfortunately, the stopper was at some point cut down and is flat on top. It should have a point similar to the stopper in photo 3127. The amount of overlay left on the edge of each panel can vary significantly. Keep in mind that primitive cutting machinery was used in making these early pieces.

3140 CUT OVERLAY FLORAL DESIGN COLOGNE

9" H. x 4½" Dia. 1850–1870

A band of daisy-like flowers surrounds this elegant cologne near the base. Leaves are cut into the ring on the neck, repeating the small leaves on the vine between the flowers. All of the Sandwich colognes with long, slender necks have this ring. It was used as a thumb and finger rest when pouring out the contents, and, when the bottle was carried, it took the weight off the lip. A polished pontil mark is on the base. The blown stopper matches the bottle in color and form, and seats properly in the throat of the bottle. The familiar Sandwich quatrefoil, seen frequently on lamps, is cut into the stopper. Because the green outer casing is thin, the cutting appears to be well executed.

3141 CUT OVERLAY COLOGNE

9⅞" H. x 3⅝" Dia. 1848–1870

On occasion, a cologne like this will be found that is cut into a random, almost haphazard design. Several different size cutting wheels were used to carve away the blue outer layer of glass. Some of the ovals are vertical, some are horizontal, and they vary in size. If you should find a bottle like this, study the shape of the bottle and the stopper for identification. The cut designs vary from bottle to bottle and cannot be used for positive ID. The stopper, blown into a mold, has a hollow core. Sometimes the top of the stopper was cut away, and the remaining glass was reshaped into a tulip by cutting the scallops into it. This stopper is numbered to match the cologne. *On loan to Sandwich Glass Museum, Sandwich Historical Society from the Hollander Family Collection*

3142 CUT OVERLAY COLOGNE WITH TULIP STOPPER

8⅛" H. x 3" Dia. 1850–1870

This cologne is without question a magnificent bottle in shape and design, but detailed study reveals poor workmanship. Note how erratically the blue lines run up the cologne, wide in some areas and almost nonexistent on the neck. The blue outer layer of glass varies in thickness, and the cutter did not compensate. Keep in mind that the goal of the cutter was to make the cologne highly desirable—as quickly as possible. In this way, he maintained high productivity. Originally, the stopper was similar to 3141, with an airtrap in the center. The top was cut away and the remainder was shaped into scallops. Ovals were cut to repeat the design of the bottle. Do not confuse the construction of this cut stopper with the lily stopper, which was pressed. *Courtesy, Sandwich Glass Museum, Sandwich Historical Society*

3143 CUT OVERLAY COLOGNE WITH SIGNED TULIP STOPPER

10" H. x 3¾" Dia. 1850

George Franklin Lapham joined the Boston and Sandwich Glass Company at age fourteen to learn the art of glass cutting. He was twenty-eight when he cut this bottle. It is in the private collection of the Lapham family and is one of the most striking examples of cutting done in Sandwich. Note the depth of the punty that makes up the inside of the four rings near the base. The rings alternate with four panels of Strawberry Diamond. This cologne was made five years after the company began to obtain sand from the Berkshire Mountains in Massachusetts. To understand how the quality of this sand changed the quality of the cutting, read about the Cheshire, Massachusetts, sand in Volume 2. We have also seen this piece in blue. Note the copper wheel engraving in the long panels below the ring on the neck.

3144 SIGNED STOPPER FROM ABOVE COLOGNE

This exquisite tulip stopper matches the cologne in every way, and if broken would greatly diminish its value. Note the teardrop running into the body of the stopper. The plug is signed "F. Lapham 1850". Mr. Lapham was known as Frank.

3145 CUT OVERLAY COLOGNE
10¼" H. x 3½" Dia. 1850–1870
The cut design of punties and diamonds is often seen on
Sandwich pieces. When it is found on pressed tableware,
the pattern is known as Diamond Thumbprint. Note the
four large pointed arches that make up the design at the
base of the bottle. This motif was repeated on the rim by
cutting it into a pointed quatrefoil, which could be seen
by looking straight down from the top. The reinforcing
ring has four V-grooves to match the design of the lip. The
matching stopper number, as well as its cut design, prove
that the stopper is original. It is lighter in color than the
bottle because the ruby layer of glass is very thin. This
change in tone does not affect the value of this magnificent
piece. *Courtesy, Sandwich Glass Museum, Sandwich Historical
Society*

3146 CUT OVERLAY COLOGNE
11⅜" H. x 4" Dia. 1850–1870
Note the slender lines of this blown molded blank. Characteristic of Sandwich colognes are the ring around the neck
for reinforcement and the slender neck that opens down
and out to become the body of the bottle. The cut design
generally changes at the widest point of the body and extends onto the bottom. A star is cut into the bottom so that
every surface of the blank is cut and polished. The design
of the bottle is repeated on an original stopper, and also
changes at the widest point. The lip is cut into six points.
The slightest nick on even one of the points will decrease
the value of the piece by more than 50 percent. *Courtesy,
Sandwich Glass Museum, Sandwich Historical Society*

3147 CUT OVERLAY COLOGNE
11½" H. x 3½" Dia. 1850–1870

This piece deserves detailed study. The neck of the bottle has five horizontal rows of punties above the reinforcing ring, with six punties in each row. This motif is repeated in the five rows below the ring. At this point the design completely changes. There are six vesicas cut into each of the next ten rows. Each vesica is longer from point to point to maintain the design as the neck widens. The design changes again, as the vesicas give way to diamonds and punties. The cuts are deeper, taking away a greater proportion of the red layer of glass. Around the base is a leaf design. The leaf design and the rows of vesicas are repeated on the stopper, which is inscribed with the same number that is inscribed on the rim of the bottle. We stress the importance of maintaining a matching stopper, and here is an excellent example. If this stopper were lost or broken, the cologne would have very little value.

3148 CUT OVERLAY VESICA COLOGNE
6⅛" H. x 4⅛" Dia. 1859–1869

This cologne belonged to Ida Nye Lloyd, daughter-in-law of James Lloyd, Deming Jarves' color expert. It was made when Lloyd was at the Cape Cod Glass Works in Sandwich. The design consists of eight vesicas: four with a Strawberry Diamond motif, two with sunbursts and two with ovals. The intricate cutting and long hours of labor indicate that this was not a production piece. The vesica with oval is repeated four times on the stopper, which is inscribed with a number that matches the number inscribed on the bottle. Sandwich colognes of this quality had as much attention paid to the base as was paid to the rest of the piece. A mark of good design is beauty when viewed from any angle. *On loan to Sandwich Glass Museum, Sandwich Historical Society from the Hollander Family Collection*

3149 CUT OVERLAY STAR IN FROSTED OVAL COLOGNE

4½" H. without stopper; 2½" Dia. 1850–1870

Overlay glass is made by taking a gather of colored glass and blowing it into a shell mold. Immediately a second gather of transparent glass is inserted into the mold and blown. The two layers, now fused together, are reheated. This gather is then blown into the mold that will shape the piece. Single overlay was called *plated*. If a total of three layers of glass were blown into the shell mold, the result was double overlay, *or double plated*. The design of this cutting is most interesting, and without question is unique to Sandwich. It is made up of four crosses alternating with four large punties. A small punty is above and below each cross, as well as a frosted oval with a cut eight-pointed star. Additional cutting was done on the neck and shoulder, and under the base there is a large polished pontil mark. The stopper is a replacement, and is not Sandwich. *Courtesy, Sandwich Glass Museum, Sandwich Historical Society*

3150 CUT OVERLAY STAR IN FROSTED PANEL COLOGNE

6⅝" H. x 2½" Dia. 1850–1870

Note the similarity in the cutting of the red panel to the overall cutting of the cologne in 3149. There are four panels with the punty and cross design, alternating with four frosted panels. Four eight-pointed stars are cut and polished into the frosted panels, but they are not precisely spaced. The cut panels on the neck and shoulder are irregular. The blown stopper matches in design, and is probably the best example of why an original stopper should be retained. If you lose the stopper, 50 percent of the value of the cologne would be lost. The blue stopper is similar, but is cut into six rather than eight panels. There are punties in the blue panels, but no crosses. *Courtesy, Sandwich Glass Museum, Sandwich Historical Society*

3151 CUT OVERLAY STAR IN FROSTED PANEL COLOGNE STOPPERS

(a) Eight panels, from above cologne
(b) Six panels 1850–1870

In most cases, highly sophisticated stoppers which match their colognes in color, design, and quality are impossible to replace. Therefore, they should be handled with great care. Note the similarity of the two stoppers. The red one is cut into eight panels. The four red panels have a punty and cross design. The blue stopper has six panels with no crosses. Yet it is obvious that the stopper blanks were alike, and the variation was created in the cutting shop. *Courtesy, Sandwich Glass Museum, Sandwich Historical Society*

3152 CUT OVERLAY PANEL AND STAR COLOGNES
7¼" H. x 2¾" Dia. 1850–1870

Stoppered pieces that have been paired from the time they were originally purchased from the glass company are often numbered consecutively. On this pair, the number 10 is on the base of one bottle and a corresponding 10 is on the plug of its stopper. The other cologne has the number 11 on both units. If the original intent had been to have an exact matching pair, the blanks would have been blown from the same batches of clear and colored glass into the same mold, and one cutter would execute the design on all four units. Seldom will you find Sandwich cut colognes of this quality that do not have a design cut into the base, even though it cannot be seen when the bottle is in an upright position. Other factories made this cologne in pressed glass with a matching pressed stopper. Sometimes they *stained* the panels, shoulder, and neck in blue or red, making the cologne look like Sandwich cut Overlay.

3153 CUT PANEL AND STAR COLOGNE
7¼" H. x 2¾" Dia. 1870–1887

As competition increased from the Midwest, the Boston and Sandwich Glass Company decreased the cost of the cologne by leaving off the outer layer of colored glass and using a clear glass faceted stopper. The design, however, was cut with the same high level of skill. The price list accompanying the 1874 catalog, now in the care of the Sandwich Historical Society, identifies the design. It was cut into eight different size bottles. Each "star" is a rayed design that fills each square. There are three horizontal rows of rayed squares on each bottle. The height of the rows of panels varies with the height of each size bottle.

3154 CUT OVERLAY OCTAGON DIAMOND COLOGNE
7¾" H. x 3" Dia. 1860–1887

Octagon Diamond is the original factory name given to this cut glass design, as recorded in the Boston and Sandwich Glass Company price list of the 1870's. Eight panels cut into the neck leave red overlay to define their sides. Four concentric rings are cut around the shoulder, accentuating a circular, red design which greatly enhances the cologne. The Octagon Diamond design that covers the body can be seen in the factory catalog on several differently shaped colognes. It was also made in blue and, rarest of all, in green. This design was also made at the Mount Washington Glass Company in New Bedford, where it was called *Two Cut Octagon Diamond*. The Mount Washington pieces do not have the stepped concentric rings surrounding the shoulder. Other glass companies made this design in a pressed pattern.

3155 CUT OVERLAY STRAWBERRY DIAMOND AND FAN COLOGNE
6" H. x 2½" Dia. 1859–1869

This is an exceptionally fine piece of glass cut at the Cape Cod Glass Company. It was extensively reproduced in France in five sizes, from two to sixteen ounces. On this original Cape Cod piece, note the uneven cutting in the Strawberry Diamond design near the base, and the uneven cutting in the fans. The colored glass left between the panels cut into the neck and shoulder varies in width. If you find this cologne with excellent, even cuttings, be wary of a reproduction. A star was cut into the base of this Cape Cod bottle after the pontil mark was polished. The original stopper was cut with fifty-four facets, and is numbered to match the bottle.

3156 CUT OVERLAY STAR IN FROSTED PANEL COLOGNE
6½" H. x 3½" Dia. 1850–1870

At one time, this bottle was a pink blank, because only the outer pink layer of glass could be seen. After it was shaped and annealed, it was sent to the cutting shop to have the outer layer cut away in the predetermined design shown here. Note the panel with four round punties. There are four red panels on the bottle, but only three matching panels with punties on the stopper. Three eight-pointed stars are cut and polished in the four frosted panels, matching three frosted panels in the stopper. The hexagonal stopper that was used as a blank can be seen on the Ring and Star cologne in photo 3102.

3157 CUT OVERLAY STAR IN FROSTED OVAL COLOGNE

10¼" H. x 3¾" Dia. 1850–1870

This cologne was given to the Sandwich Glass Museum by a descendant of the Holway family. It had been given to the Holways by Charlotte Hall Chipman, the granddaughter of gaffer Charles W. Lapham, who had gathered the first piece of glass for the Sandwich Glass Manufactory on July 4, 1825. Many Sandwich colognes have this shape. Note the ring around the slender neck. It was used as a thumb and finger rest to facilitate carrying and pouring. Eight-pointed stars are cut into the large frosted ovals near the base. This design is repeated four times, giving the cologne a square appearance. The two rows of punties cut into the stopper match the rows of punties on the neck above the ring. The stopper and bottle have matching numbers. *Courtesy, Sandwich Glass Museum, Sandwich Historical Society*

3158 CUT DOUBLE OVERLAY COLOGNE

2" H. x 1¼" Dia. 1850–1870

In 1947, when digging near the Lower House, we discovered this little cologne with its broken stopper 3½' underground. Although whole pieces are rarely found at the site, this bottle is a rare and perfect exception. The stopper is unfinished—it broke in the process of fitting it to the bottle. If the stopper had been the only one left made from the same batch of glass, and it broke, it may have rendered the bottle useless, accounting for its being discarded. Note the cross and four punties that were cut into the stopper. This design is closely related to several Overlay colognes shown in this chapter. Careful study of cut designs will soon enable you to identify those from Sandwich. There is a layer of white glass under the layer of deep pink. At the time this bottle was made, double Overlay was called *doubled plated*. A Boston and Sandwich Glass Company statement dated December 14, 1849, lists "3 dozen double plated double cut colognes" for $2.50 a dozen.

3159 CUT DOUBLE OVERLAY VINTAGE GRAPE COLOGNE

4⅞" H. x 2" Dia. 1850–1870

The arches cut into the side of this bottle are the simplest form of cut designs, easy to execute and pleasing to the eye. The design is delineated by the layer of white glass between the pink and the clear. The leaves of the copper wheel engraved, Vintage Grape design are frosted, while the grapes were polished for added clarity. There are three bunches of grapes, maintaining the three-panel motif that is characteristic of engraved and decorated ware at Sandwich. These grapes are nestled among the leaves, but some cutters would "hang" the grapes away from the leaves, attaching them to the vine by a twig. A horizontal line separates the design on the body from the design on the neck and shoulder. There is a sixteen point star cut into the base. The stopper has a six petal rosette on top, and is matching numbered. Sometimes Overlay colognes were marketed with clear lapidary stoppers. Make sure the numbers match. *On loan to Sandwich Glass Museum, Sandwich Historical Society from the Hollander Family Collection*

3160 RUBY STAINED VINTAGE GRAPE COLOGNES

(a) Light Stain 6¾" H. x 2½" Dia.
(b) Dark Stain 6½" H. x 2½" Dia. 1880–1887

These colognes were stained with a solution that was painted on the glass after it was annealed. They were then put into a decorating kiln and fired to make the stain permanent. There is a significant difference in the color of the two colognes. It was sometimes claimed that the amount of use would drastically change the color, so that the one on the left would be considered well used, while the cologne on the right remained little used and unwashed. A study of the light piece shows that none of the stain has wear. It was stained with a weaker solution than the cologne on the right, and has always been lighter. Note also the raised bases. Ruby stained glass is frequently thought as being Bohemian in manufacture. However, as we will see, the same technique was used in the manufacture of ruby stained glass at the Boston and Sandwich Glass Company.

3161 RUBY STAINED VINTAGE GRAPE COLOGNE

7½" H. x 3" Dia. 1880–1887

This cologne has a flat base instead of the raised base seen in most. Colognes in the ruby stained series have acid-etched leaves and polished grapes. This is a good clue that they were made at the Boston and Sandwich Glass Company, and not in Bohemia. (This applies, however, only to *ruby* stained items.) The grapes were polished back through the stain to provide some sparkle to an otherwise dull piece. The fragments were dug at the factory site. The stoppers and colognes that we have studied *in the inexpensive ruby stained series* were *not* inscribed with numbers.

3162 RUBY STAINED VINTAGE GRAPE COLOGNES

(a) Ring-necked, flat base 6½" H. x 2½" Dia.
(b) No ring, raised base 7" H. x 2½" Dia.
(c) No ring, raised base 6¾" H. x 2½" Dia.
    1880–1887

Each cologne was made from a different mold, yet each holds the same amount of liquid. Expect great variations in shape, and radical differences in staining patterns. Note the varied shapes of the leaves acid-etched onto the colognes. The cologne in the center has a long, narrow neck, while the bottle on the right obviously has a shorter, wide neck, again reflecting the great variety of shapes you may encounter.

3163 RUBY STAINED VINTAGE GRAPE COLOGNE
8" H. x 4" Dia. 1880–1887

This is the largest cologne in the ruby stained series. The two rings surrounding the shoulder were part of the mold and were not applied. An intricate design of acid-etched leaves and polished grapes surrounds the body of the cologne, and, below, a chain of cut punties encircles the piece at its widest point. An acid-etched vine below the punties repeats the design in miniature. A slightly raised base completes the bottle.

3164 RUBY STAINED COPPER WHEEL ENGRAVED COLOGNE
5¾" H. x 2½" Dia. 1880–1887

Ruby stained glass was made in many shapes and sizes. The design, copper wheel engraved into this cologne, is unique but matches many fragments that were dug at the Boston and Sandwich Glass Company. The tiny ovals engraved into the corners of the plaid design make each square resemble the German cross of the pressed tableware pattern known as Sandwich Star. But note the bottom square to the left of center. In the hasty manner of workmanship in the dying years of the company, the engraver left out one tiny oval. The stopper is not original. It does not match the cologne in form and color and descends too far into the throat.

3165 RUBY STAINED CUT COLOGNES
7½" H. x 3½" Dia. 1880–1887

One of the most sought after colors in the late era at Sandwich was red. The most inexpensive method for making clear glass red was to stain it. Great quantities of ruby stained glass were produced at the Boston and Sandwich Glass Company, and, on rare occasions, pieces can be found in amber and blue. This pair of bottles was made and annealed, after which punties and vesicas were cut to give them a design. The red stain was then brushed on between the cut designs, overlapping into the cut areas. This gave the illusion of depth. The stain overlap can be mistaken for the outer layer of glass on Overlay pieces. Then they were placed in a kiln and fired to fix the color.

3166 RUBY STAINED MORNING GLORY LEAF COLOGNE

7½" H. x 3½" Dia. 1880-1887

The Bohemian influence on the Sandwich glass industry can be seen in many pieces of ruby stained glass. But Sandwich had the knack of combining the Bohemian method with designs that were used on American glass, such as in the leaf made famous on Morning Glory pressed pattern tableware. Leaves on the same vine point in opposite directions and there are no flowers. The ovoids below the vine are common to both American and Bohemian work. *Courtesy, Sandwich Glass Museum, Sandwich Historical Society*

3167 OVERSHOT COLOGNE

8" H.; 2½" square at base 1870-1887

The glass we call Overshot today was marketed as Frosted Ware by the Boston and Sandwich Glass Company. The square colognes shown here can be seen in an original factory catalog from the 1870's. They were made in five sizes and could be purchased singly or as two units of a three-piece toilet set. We seldom find one with its original Overshot stopper, because it has usually been replaced by a clear faceted one. Overshot was made by applying clear ground glass particles to a hot gather of glass either before or after it had been shaped. The finished product appeared to be cool and frosty, accounting for its name.

3168 OVERSHOT COLOGNE

5⅝" H.; 2" square at base 1870-1887

This excellent cologne shows how color was achieved in the making of Overshot. A thin layer of colored glass (in this instance, deep pink) was used to case the inside of both the bottle and the stopper. Proof of this can be seen in the neck. When the throat of the bottle was polished to fit the stopper, the inside layer of pink was taken away, returning the neck to clear glass. On the stopper, the pink inner casing can easily be seen just above the lip of the bottle. For more information on Overshot, see Chapter 6 of Volume 4. *Courtesy, Sandwich Glass Museum, Sandwich Historical Society*

**3169 ACID-ETCHED FANNED IN FERN GLOBE
COLOGNE**
3⅝" H. x 2½" Dia. 1870–1887
The 1874 Boston and Sandwich Glass Company catalog
shows blown globe colognes in eight sizes. This one
appears to be the smallest. The stopper was pressed in a
mold and then cut into diamond-shaped facets. A star cut
into the top of the stopper matches the star cut into the
base of the bottle. After careful study, you will be able to
recognize Sandwich pieces even if you have not previously
seen that particular piece. This cologne relates in shape to
photo 4207 and is identical in design to photo 4203.

**3170 COPPER WHEEL ENGRAVED BAND AND
LINE WITH GRAPES COLOGNE**
5" H. x 1½" Dia. 1875–1887
The grape design was a popular one during the Late
Blown Period at Sandwich. A matching design can be seen
on the slop bowl in photo 4209 in Volume 4. Eight panels
were cut into the neck of the bottle. A polished pontil mark
is on the underside. Gilded bands surround the cologne,
and the gilding was carried onto the panels of the stopper,
which is numbered to match. This stopper is closely identified with the New England Glass Company, but can be
found on several documented Sandwich colognes. Remember, we cannot always attribute a particular shape to only
one company, because several companies used the same
shaped molds.

3171 THREADED COLOGNE
5⅜" H. x 2⅛" Dia. 1880–1887

Many times in the study of glass we find a design that is the essence of beauty and simplicity. By threading just the stopper and the bottom half of this cologne, and calling it complete, a worker made this piece one of the finest examples of Sandwich workmanship. The plain bottles that were used as blanks for Threaded Glass can be seen in the 1874 Boston and Sandwich Glass Company factory catalog. The bottle, stopper, and threading were made from the same batch of green glass. The stopper is inscribed with a number matching that on the cologne. See Chapter 13 in Volume 4 for information about the threading of glass.
Courtesy, Sandwich Glass Museum, Sandwich Historical Society

3172 THREADED COLOGNE WITH ENGRAVED IVY AND BERRIES
6¼" H. x 2½" Dia. 1880–1887

The threading on Sandwich pieces starts at the pontil mark and in most cases continues one-third up the side. The upper part remains clear. In this cologne, an ivy vine with groups of three berries was copper wheel engraved on the unthreaded section. Do not limit your thinking to a particular engraved or etched design. Study the shape of the bottle, as well as the method of threading, and accept *any* design in the unthreaded part. An attempt to cut ovals into the threads of the stopper was not successful, and the threads shattered. The stopper does not appear to match the bottle, which has no ovals cut into it. However, both pieces are inscribed with identical numbers. *Courtesy, Sandwich Glass Museum, Sandwich Historical Society*

3173 THREADED GLOBE COLOGNE
4½" H. without stopper; 3¼" Dia. 1880–1887

It is not often that we find Sandwich pieces completely threaded. It took more time, more glass, and added little to the value of the piece. Normally, the threading stops about one-third up the side of the bottle, where the threading in the photo looks the darkest. The neck was cut into panels that continue down to the shoulder. There are two clues that the stopper is a replacement. First, it does not match the cologne in size. The original was probably threaded and was larger. Second, a number is inscribed on the bottle, but there is no number on the stopper.
Courtesy, Sandwich Glass Museum, Sandwich Historical Society

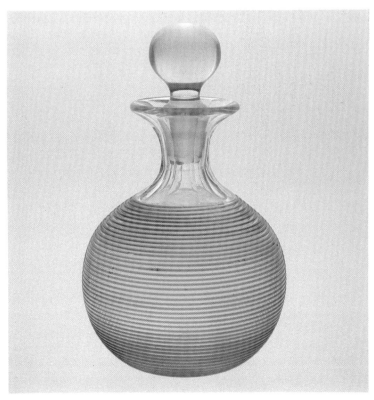

INVENTORY OF SANDWICH GLASS

No.	Description	Condition	Date Purchased	Amount	Date Sold	Amount

A STUDY OF STOPPERS

Stoppers excavated at the site of the Boston and Sandwich Glass Company 1825–1887

As mundane as they may seem, stoppers have just as much importance as the bottles they protect.

To the serious collector, a bottle is not truly complete unless it is surmounted either with its original stopper, or, if the original has been lost, with a stopper of the period which displays the style, the color (if any), and the proportions which the glassmaker intended.

An original stopper can increase the market value of a bottle by as much as four times. Conversely, without a correct stopper, a bottle can command only half the price or less.

So the serious glass student will expend as much effort in getting the right stopper as in finding the perfect bottle.

Because stoppers are somewhat homely items compared to the richness of design and manufacture of decanters or colognes, little attention has been given to their identification and to the niceties of their manufacture. The problem has been compounded by the fact that stoppers, like bottles of various types, were widely copied by New England manufacturers among each other and from European sources.

Because they were relatively cheap to make and were manufactured in vast quantities, the collector becomes further confused. Stoppers which fell to the floor during manufacture were not considered worth retrieving, so they were swept into the dump literally by the thousands. Collectors and the curious acquired cartons of them by picking the site of the Boston and Sandwich Glass Company. The fragment collection of Francis (Bill) Wynn, who was well known to the glass research field, contained 752 stoppers. Four hundred were included in the Casey fragment collection. Gradually, these collections and several others were added to our Barlow collection, representing more than eight thousand perfect stoppers and five hundred pounds of stopper fragments (If this amount of stoppers had been discarded by the factory because of no apparent salvage value, think of the enormous amount which must have been made and shipped).

Because so many American and foreign glass companies copied each other's stopper designs, we are reluctantly con-vinced that a bottle cannot be attributed to a specific glass house on the basis of its stopper design *alone*.

However, all of the stoppers shown in this chapter came from the Boston and Sandwich Glass Company dump site. We can therefore say, without too much fear of contradiction, that any stoppers you have which match these are at least of the period (assuming they are not obvious reproductions), that they could have been made at Sandwich, and that your ability to identify what you have, based on the text and illustrations herein, brings you closer to the attribution of the total piece than you might otherwise have achieved.

At the very least, we hope that the information on stoppers will provide you with some interesting insights which have not heretofore been available.

Stopper production began on the first full day of glassmaking at the Sandwich Glass Manufactory on July 9, 1825. Toy decanters were made, which took small loosely fitting hand-formed ball stoppers and Sunburst stoppers, which were called *star stoppers* in the factory sloar book. During the first month, Sunburst stoppers for quart decanters were made, as were flathead stoppers and stoppers for cruets. Sixty-eight large flathead stoppers *for initialling* are listed in November 1825. This original company document finally dispels the myth that Sandwich glassmaking had a shaky beginning because they had to use local sand from a pile in the factory yard!

As glass production increased, so did the stopper count. By the time the Sandwich Glass Manufactory became incorporated as the Boston and Sandwich Glass Company, over one thousand stoppers were being made each week in one shop at the eight-pot furnace. These early stoppers were free-blown, blown molded or formed by hand from a solid glob of glass.

Every glass factory that manufactured containers in the early 1800's may not have made accompanying stoppers, because the Sandwich factory sloar book reveals that Sandwich produced stoppers to be shipped out to other factories. Records indicate great numbers of stoppers were made compared to the numbers of containers that they would fit. For example, during the week of March 15, 1828, Michael Doyle's shop made 150 quart three-ring decanters and 387 no-ring decanters—a total of less than six hundred decanters. The rest of the time Doyle's shop made lamps and dishes. The other shops around the furnace made witch balls, champagnes, lemonades, tumblers, wines, lamp globes, some cruets which took stoppers, some caster bottles which may or may not have taken stoppers, and peppers which did not. Compare this to the more than one thousand stoppers that were produced during the same week. In the shop of Samuel Barnes, one man was asked to stay, after he had completed his regular work, to make 301 cruet stoppers, 305 ball stoppers, 228 more cruet stoppers, and 312 half-pint cruet stoppers. Samuel Kern made 178 mushroom stoppers and George Hartshorn made ninety-one ball stoppers. Over 1500 stoppers were produced, yet during the same time period only 750 items that would take a stopper were made. If this was an occasional occurrence it would have no significance, but between 1825 and 1828 this practice continued week after week, doubling, tripling, and sometimes quadrupling the number of stoppers produced compared with the number of items in which a stopper could be used. It is very clear that the factory was either stockpiling great quantities for future use, or they were selling them to other glass factories. If the latter is true, it means that Sandwich stoppers may be fitted to containers that were made at other glass houses. The unanswered questions that arise from research of this magnitude can be frustrating, but our feeling is that the earliest decanters and cruets *cannot* be attributed to a particular glass factory on the basis of the shape, pattern, or cutting of the stopper alone.

As pressing techniques were perfected in the 1830's, stoppers were made by forcing the hot glass with a plunger into a mold that consisted of a rectangular reservoir connected to three or four stopper-shaped cavities. This mold produced a block of glass with the stoppers attached to it at their plug ends. After the glass was removed from the mold, the stoppers were broken away from the block of glass. The block of glass was returned to the cullet shop, where it was stored until it was remelted in another batch of metal. The use of this block mold increased production, but did not curtail the blowing of stoppers. Unlike production methods for other styles and patterns of Sandwich-made articles that can be related to various time periods, each new method in stopper technology was carried on *in addition* to older methods. The simplest ball stopper was blown molded from the first days of production to the last, with improvements on the plug end to help distinguish among them.

By the 1840's, another improvement in the pressing of stoppers came into use. On August 6, 1841, Hiram Dillaway, a mold maker who would later become head of the Boston and Sandwich Glass Company machine shop and engine room, sent to the United States Patent Office specifications for a mold designed to revolutionize stopper pressing. His "new and useful improvement in the art of pressing solid articles of glassware in molds" allowed up to twenty-four stoppers to be made at the same time.

Dillaway's patent replaced the rectangular block with a cylinder that he called a *fountain* (see Dillaway's patent). Each stopper form radiated from and was connected by its plug end to the center fountain, the way spokes radiate from the hub of a wheel. A plunger forced the molten glass into the fountain, and then into each stopper form. After the wheel of stoppers was removed from the mold, the stoppers were broken away from the center hub by tapping them with a mallet. If a stopper bounced to the floor instead of into the stopper bin, it was not worth retrieving. This is why so many stoppers are dug at the site that still have mold marks on the side of the plug. The mold marks on the plug of stoppers found at the site are proof that the stoppers were manufactured by the Boston and Sandwich Glass Company, and were not discarded after use by the townspeople or brought into the factory as part of a load of purchased cullet. After the stoppers were broken away, the glass that made up the hub was stored for later use as cullet.

As noted previously, minutes of the June 6, 1846, Board of Directors' meeting record an accusation by the New England Glass Company that the Boston and Sandwich Glass Company was infringing on a stopper patent. Several times throughout the history of both companies, this claim was made in regard to other aspects of glass-making—the pressing of knobs and the making of silvered glass (mercury glass). Recurring claims of patent infringement seemed to be a normal part of the glass business that sometimes caused no more than a minor irritation. But more detail in this instance is needed to show why the attribution of glass can be difficult.

Hiram Dillaway, around whom much of the patent controversy swirled, was born in Uxbridge, Massachusetts, in 1813. At the age of fifteen, he served for one year as an apprentice to E. M. Bartholomew, a South Boston mold maker. His apprenticeship began on August 26, 1828. His early career during the following ten year period is not clear. He did renew his apprenticeship with Bartholomew.

Wooden patterns of block molds from the Boston and Sandwich Glass Company. These patterns were sent to the foundry as the first step in casting the molds in which stoppers would be made.

Hiram Dillaway, who trained under a Boston mold maker, became head of the machine shop and engine room. *Courtesy, Sandwich Glass Museum, Sandwich Historical Society*

Boston and Sandwich Glass Company machine shop. *On loan to Sandwich Glass Museum, Sandwich Historical Society by Carol Morrow*

He is not listed as being in business for himself in the Boston Business Directory, but one Enoch S. Dillaway is listed as a brass founder as early as 1827, and as a machinist by 1838. Dillaway family papers state that Hiram Dillaway came to Sandwich from the "Mount Washington Glass Manufactory". Deming Jarves established his Mount Washington works in 1837. It appears likely that after Hiram Dillaway left Bartholomew he worked with Enoch Dillaway, then spent a year in Mount Washington. The earliest records placing Dillaway in Sandwich are both dated December 1838. The marriage of Hiram Dillaway of Sandwich to Mary Le(h)man of Boston was announced in the *Barnstable Patriot, and Commercial Advertiser* dated December 19, 1838, and, according to payroll records preserved by the Sandwich Historical Society, he is first listed on the factory payroll for the period of December 17–29, 1838. Although Hiram and Mary Dillaway made their home in Sandwich, and over the next several years their three children were born in Sandwich, it appears that Dillaway himself may have returned to Boston. He had come to Sandwich at a time when the glass industry was in deep trouble, following the financial panic of 1837. In 1839, the Board of Directors of the Boston and Sandwich Glass Company discussed severing connections with the factory in Sandwich and ordering Superintendent William Stutson not to fill the pots. On March 26, 1840, the *Yarmouth Register* announced with regret the suspension of glassmaking due to "difficulties of the times". The name of Hiram Dillaway was removed from the company payroll.

On August 6, 1841, when Dillaway patented his stopper mold, his address was given as Boston. He could have

been with Enoch S. Dillaway, who in later years would list his address as 51 Federal Street, the building that housed the offices of all of Deming Jarves' enterprises. Or, he could have returned to the Jarves-owned factory in South Boston that was called the Mount Washington Glass Manufactory, later to become the Mount Washington Glass Works.

As a private individual who was granted a patent, Hiram Dillaway was free to allow one or several companies, including the New England Glass Company, to press stoppers by his improved method. Possibly by 1843, and definitely by 1845, Dillaway once again settled in Sandwich — this time permanently. The Boston and Sandwich Glass Company had access to Dillaway's brilliance, and the New England Glass Company may have resented it.

Some time after the New England Glass Company made the 1846 accusation of patent infringement, both companies tried to come to terms with each other and with Dillaway, but records from May and June 1848, say that a legal problem arose regarding the purchase of Dillaway's patent for stoppers by the Boston and Sandwich Glass Company "and others". The outcome was hazy in the minutes of the Board of Directors' meetings, but on May 1, 1855, the patent was reissued to private citizen Hiram Dillaway of Sandwich, Massachusetts.

In 1865, Dillaway worked under contract for the Cape Cod Glass Company while he was still on salary at the Boston and Sandwich Glass Company. It appears that he did not assign his patents to any one company, but continued to collect royalties for his inventions. Eventually many glass companies in New England and in the Pittsburgh area adopted the Dillaway method of pressing stoppers without paying royalties. It took little change in mold construction for a glass company to circumvent a patent right.

Some of the stoppers dug from the factory site were inscribed with a number. This was common practice for better quality pieces. After a stopper was fitted to a bottle, both units were inscribed with the same number, allowing the finished stopper to travel through the factory and be packaged and shipped with its intended bottle at the end. It would be an oversimplification to say that, if a bottle and its stopper have matching numbers, it is Sandwich. Unfortunately for Sandwich collectors, many glass houses in this country and abroad used this system. But regardless of which company made a certain piece, finding the same number on a bottle and its stopper helps to determine that the stopper is original. This is particularly important if the decanter, oil bottle, or cologne you are buying is or was one of a pair. If you are buying a single piece, such as a decanter, and the seller has two, make sure that the stoppers have not been accidentally switched. An ill-fitting stopper with a different number greatly decreases the value of the bottle. Your money is invested much more wisely when you purchase the pair rather than convince the owner to sell you only one. Items that were originally sold in pairs, such as matching decanters, candlesticks, and vases, are more valuable today when they are kept as pairs. For example, if a cologne is valued at $100, and a second identical $100 cologne can be matched to it, another $100 is added for a total value of $300.

Generally, the numbers inscribed at the factory are quite legible. Occasionally a piece is found with both numbers identical but very poorly executed. The last two sentences of the following magazine article explain why. The article was taken from an issue of *Peterson's*, probably issued in October 1872.

> To Take Stoppers Out of Bottles and Decanters. — Take the bottle or decanter by the neck with the left hand, and place the first finger at the back of the stopper. Take a piece of wood in the right hand, and tap the stopper first one side, then the other, turning the decanter round in the hand. A quick succession of little, short taps is the most effective. If this plan fails, wind a bit of rough string once around the neck, one end of the string being held by one person, the other by another; pull backward and forward till the neck becomes hot with friction. Then tap as before. Stoppers often become wedged into decanters from the wrong stopper being used. To avoid this the bottom of the stopper should be scratched with a number, and a corresponding number scratched under the bottom of the decanter.

There is one type of stopper that is today called a *cover*, so we have not dealt with it at length in this study. This is the upper unit that was fitted to wide-mouthed jars for pickles, spices, and medicinal salts. Catalogs illustrate medicine jars, square in shape, that were called *medicine squares*. They had a large opening for contents that were not liquid, such as smelling salts, lavender salts, and other pharmaceuticals. This large opening was called a *salt mouth*. It took a cover with a deep inner rim that fit inside the wide neck of the jar. The outside of the inner rim was roughly ground to make a tight fit in the same manner as our spice jars of today. These jars were listed as "stoppered", not covered. Regardless of their diameter, a cover that was machined to fit like the plug of a stopper was called a *stop*.

THESE SIMPLE HINTS WILL HELP YOU IDENTIFY SANDWICH STOPPERS.

The reprint of the Boston and Sandwich Glass Company 1874 catalog is your best friend. Study the stoppered pieces to learn the type of stopper that was original to each piece.

Study the shapes of the blanks used for cutting and engraving. Although variations occur among different cutters, the shape of the original blank is the determining clue to its having been made at Sandwich.

United States Patent Office.

HIRAM DILLAWAY, OF SANDWICH, MASSACHUSETTS.

IMPROVEMENT IN THE CONSTRUCTION OF MOLDS FOR PRESSING GLASS.

Specification forming part of Letters Patent No. 2,226, dated August 21, 1841; Reissue No. 308, dated May 1, 1855.

To all whom it may concern:

Be it known that I, HIRAM DILLAWAY, late of Boston, in the county of Suffolk, but now of Sandwich, in the county of Barnstable, and Commonwealth of Massachusetts, have invented a new and useful Improvement in Molds for the Manufacture of Articles of Glassware; and I do hereby declare that the following is a full and exact description of the same.

My said invention is to be found in such a formation of the mold as shall cause the forms—by which I mean the cavities—into which the articles are to be pressed or molded to be filled with the melted glass to great advantage by means of a pressure applied to a mass of that material in a larger fountain connected with the forms, and it may be applied either to pressing a single article or a number of articles at one operation.

I will describe, that mold which I have found convenient for pressing a number of small articles at once, but the relative positions of the forms may be varied according to circumstances in molding different articles so long as they are arranged so as to lead out of the lower part of the fountain. A block, of a circular or other convenient form, proportioned to the size of the article and number of them to be formed at once, is made with a central elevation or neck on the top, in diameter equal to about one-half, and in height equal to about the whole, of that of the body of the block. The block is divided horizontally through the middle so as to make an upper and lower section, which constitute the two parts of an open and shut mold. Through the center of this elevation or neck the upper section is bored vertically so as to have a cylindrical hollow, of a diameter about half of that of the neck, passing entirely through it. The lower section is also bored vertically through the center, but so as to have a bore of a diameter a little larger than that of the bore of the upper section. The lower edge of the bore of the upper section is then hollowed or grooved out so as to make it meet and match that of the lower section when the two parts are put together. All that part of the cylindrical hollow thus made through the entire block, which is not occupied by the bottom piece hereinafter described, I call the "fountain." The forms of the articles to be pressed are made by cavi-

ties on the inner surfaces of the upper and lower sections of the block cut to the shape designed, those in the upper matching with those in the lower section, and so disposed as to communicate with the central cylindrical hollow, and, when it is desirable to cast more than one article by one operation, the forms or cavities may be made to radiate or diverge from the central bore toward the outer circle of the block, as in the mold I am now describing. It may be found convenient to have in that part of the forms next to the central bore a small elevation, n n, (see the drawings hereinafter referred to,) with a sharpened edge sufficient to form a slight indentation around the end of the article pressed. These forms may be as numerous as the size of the article to be made and of the block containing them will admit, those in the mold exhibited in the drawings being for making glass stoppers for bottles. To the bore of the lower section is fitted a bottom piece, f, reaching as high as the lower edge of the forms and entirely filling the bore to that point, this bottom piece to be made movable. A plunger is fitted to the hollow in the neck of the upper section so as to pass down the bore to the bottom piece. When the plunger is brought down entirely home to the bottom piece, the diameter of the bore of the lower section being larger than that of the bore of the upper, and consequently than that of the plunger which is fitted to it, and the lower edge of this upper bore being hollowed out to meet the upper edge of the lower one, as above described, there is left around the bottom of the plunger a vacant chamber, h h, into which all the forms open, so that the plunger, however far pressed down, cannot close or obstruct the mouths of the forms. It may be found convenient to have, as in the mold I am now describing, on the inner surface of the upper section, at convenient points near its circumference, elongated square elevations, and on that of the lower one corresponding depressions, matching the one into the other, for the purpose of keeping each part of the mold secure in its proper place. The block may be made of cast-iron, or other metal sufficiently firm for the purpose and capable of bearing heat, and the central hollow and plunger may be made square, instead of cylindrical, when a number of articles are to

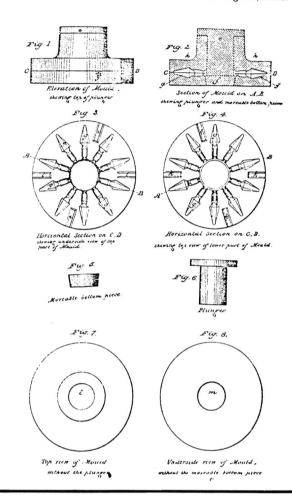

---

2   308

be made at once, of such a shape as to make that form most convenient.

For the better specification of my said improvement I refer to the accompanying drawings as follows:

Figure 1 is the block, showing the horizontal division C D, and the top of the plunger e dropped entirely down to reach the bottom piece. Fig. 2 is a vertical section of the block A B, showing the plunger e and movable bottom piece, f, and a sectional division of the forms or matrices g, and of the hollowing out of the lower edge of the bore in the upper section to meet the larger diameter of the bore in the lower section, the whole being to form the lower or auxiliary chamber, h. Figs. 3 and 4 are horizontal sections of the mold on C D, showing plan of the forms or matrices g in the inner surfaces of the upper and lower sections of the mold; also, the elevations i and depressions k. Fig. 5 is a movable bottom piece. Fig. 6 is a plunger. Fig. 7 is a top view of the mold without the plunger, showing the aperture l, into which the plunger passes. Fig. 8 is an under-side view of the mold without the movable bottom piece, and showing the aperture into which it is placed.

The mode of using my said mold is described as follows: The mold being properly heated, a quantity of metal sufficient to fill all the forms or matrices, and a portion of the central hollow or fountain besides, is gathered and dropped in at the neck of the upper section. The plunger is then brought down upon it with a pressure sufficient to force the metal out laterally from the central hollow into all the forms or matrices communicating with it. Should the quantity gathered and dropped in at any time be so little more than enough to fill the forms as to allow the plunger to be forced down below their upper edges, the metal not required to fill the forms remaining in and filling the chamber above described will be sufficient to prevent any imperfection in the pressing. After the metal is partially cooled the upper section is removed, and the pressed glass taken from the lower one, and the articles broken from the central mass at the indentations made by the edged elevation

before referred to. The object of making the bottom piece movable is that if the glass hangs or adheres to the lower section the bottom piece may be moved by force or pressure applied from below, and sufficient to start from the mold the glass with the articles attached, such being sometimes found necessary.

Any number of articles, according to their size and that of the block containing the forms, may be pressed at one time from one central fountain and by one plunger. The size, weight, and thickness of the articles made at each successive use of the same mold will be the same, the difference between the quantity of metal supplied at one time and another being left in the central mass instead of being forced into the article formed.

I claim—

1. So combining with a mold fountain or reservoir provided with a plunger, one or more matrices or molds that a liquid mass of glass, when pressed in said fountain or reservoir by the plunger, may be made to flow or pass therefrom and into such matrix or matrices.

2. Combining with a series of matrices and a press chamber or reservoir surrounded by them an auxiliary annular and concentric chamber, as seen at h h, in Fig. 2, formed in the two mold plates and made to perform the function of preventing the plunger from clogging the mouths of the matrices under circumstances as above stated, and also to prevent the chilled glass from obstructing the downward movement of the plunger.

3. So combining with the lower mold-plate a movable bottom block, f, that the same may not only serve to form a bottom to the main and auxiliary mold-chambers, or to the former, but also enable a person to detach the pressed glass or metal from the lower mold-plate under circumstances and in manner as above set forth.

In testimony whereof I have hereunto set my signature this 16th day of March, A. D. 1855.

HIRAM DILLAWAY.

Witnesses:
R. H. EDDY,
F. P. HALE, Jr.

Hiram Dillaway's patent for pressing many stoppers at one time, dated August 21, 1841, and reissued with minor improvements on May 1, 1855.

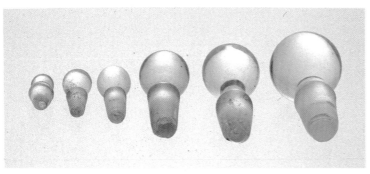

3174 HAND-FORMED BALL STOPPERS
1" H.-2" H. 1825–1828

Here is the simplest form of stopper made at Sandwich. Some have no shank—the plug is tight against the ball finial. Some have a short shank. Hand-formed ball stoppers were sometimes used on plain toy decanters, made from the first day of production at Deming Jarves' Sandwich Glass Manufactory.

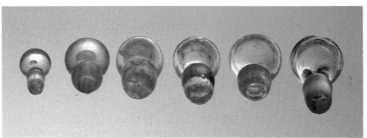

3175 FREE-BLOWN BALL STOPPERS
1" H.-2" H. 1825–1828

All six stoppers were dug at the Sandwich site. Note the size of the plugs. Five stoppers have not been machined to fit into bottles. The stopper on the right was. Did it come from a bottle shipped into the factory which was later thrown away? We can't tell for sure, but it *does* match the other stoppers in every detail.

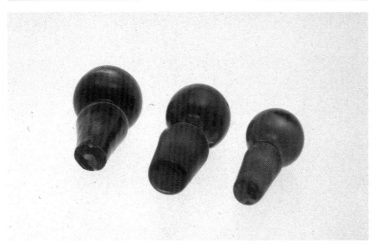

3176 BALL STOPPERS
(a) Free-blown 2" H.
(b) Pressed 2" H.
(c) Pressed 1½" H. 1830–1835

In early days, all the stoppers of this size with a ball finial were free-blown individually, and roughly pre-shaped. They required excessive machining to shape the plug, and there was always the danger of cutting into the airtrap. A normal day's production for one shop was 350 stoppers. In later years, with the advent of pressing, perfect stoppers far superior to those free-blown were turned out at the rate of one thousand per hour.

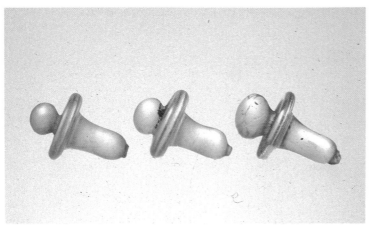

3177 HAND-FORMED TAM-O'-SHANTER STOPPERS
1½" H. 1825–1830

These are the stoppers that were used in vinegar cruets in the late 1820's. They were made in clear, blue, and amethyst. They show the individuality of each man who worked on them. Note the differences in the ball finials. The stopper in the center has no shank between the ball and the disk. All three have a pontil mark at the bottom. There are no mold marks on these early stoppers, and no airtrap in their centers, proving they were hand-formed— neither blown into a mold nor pressed.

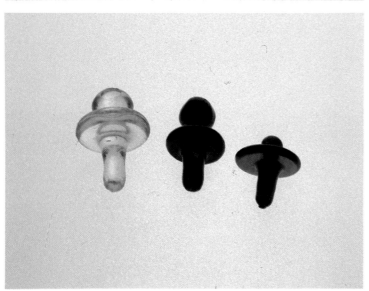

3178 HAND-FORMED TAM-O'-SHANTER STOPPERS
(a) 2" H. x 1¼" Dia.
(b) 1¾" H. x 1" Dia.
(c) 1¼" H. x ¾" Dia. 1825–1830

These stoppers show the clarity and color of the glass made in Sandwich. All three stoppers have a pontil mark on the end of the plug. The disk beneath the ball finial can vary from ¾" diameter to 1½" diameter, as shown here. These early stoppers were not made to fit individual cruets. Their only purpose was to slow down evaporation and keep dirt and insects from entering the bottle. The disk rested loosely on the rim of the bottle.

3179 HAND-FORMED RIBBED TAM-O'-SHANTER STOPPERS

(a) Plain, for comparison 2" H. x 1¼" Dia.
(b) Ribbed, large ball finial 1½" H. x 1" Dia.
(c) Ribbed, small ball finial 1¾" H. x 1⅛" Dia.
   1825–1830

All three stoppers were made at a temperature when the glass could be worked like putty. Study the plug on stopper C. The spirals are the last signs of the crimping that formed the ribs. As the plug was worked into shape, the ribs gradually disappeared.

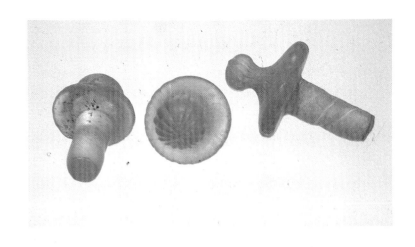

3180 FREE-BLOWN TAM-O'-SHANTER STOPPERS

(a) Plug too short 1½" H. x¾" Dia.
(b) Hole in plug 2" H. x 1" Dia. 1825–1830

When searching for a free-blown stopper, look for a plain, very smooth exterior with an airtrap in the center. Stopper A was dug at the site of the Boston and Sandwich Glass Company. It was discarded because the plug was too short for the size of the stopper and could easily fall out. Stopper B was also dug at the site, discarded because, although the plug is the proper length, it has a hole in the end. Sediment could enter the airtrap where it could not be cleaned, so the stopper became useless. It is, however, an excellent example of what was made in the earliest days of production.

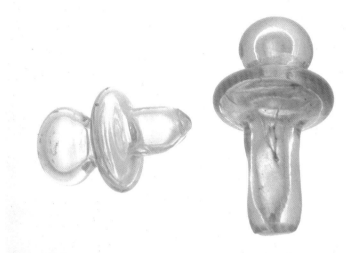

3181 BLOWN MOLDED RIBBED BALL DECANTER STOPPERS

3½" H. 1825–1830

The great number of stoppers found at the Sandwich dig site with this pattern were discarded because of a hole in the bottom of the plug, similar to the one that can be seen on the right stopper. It appears that some finish work was done on the plugs, and as the bottom was machined, they cut through to the airtrap. Because dirt and sediment could enter the plug, they were thrown away. There is no other damage. Today, finding a decanter with a stopper that has a hole in it should not affect the value of the piece.

3182 BLOWN MOLDED DECANTER STOPPERS

(a) Ridged 3¼" H.
(b) Ribbed 4" H. 1825–1830

Both stoppers were thrown away during production because holes broke through to the inside when they were disconnected from the blowpipe. The dark discoloration in stopper A is caused by sediment on the inside of the plug. Mold marks can clearly be seen on the plug of stopper B, indicating that it was never machined and completed. Today, we are satisfied to see the correct pattern stopper on an early decanter even if their is an opening into the airtrap. However, it is not the original stopper, because the Boston and Sandwich Glass Company did not ship open stoppers out of the factory. The ripples seen on the lower part of the ball of stopper A are the ridges reflected through from the other side.

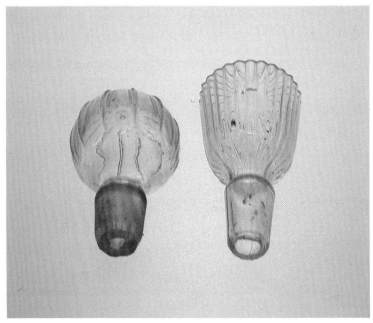

3183 PRESSED DIAMOND POINT STOPPERS
(a, b) Diamond Point 3¼" H.
(c, d) Fine Diamond Point 2" H. 1841–1850

The stoppers shown here were pressed in a Diamond Point pattern, with a smooth cap. They came from three different size wheel molds—stoppers A and B came from the same size, and stoppers C and D each came from different wheel molds. Up to twenty-four stoppers were made at one time using this method of production, but all of the stoppers on a wheel were identical in size, shape, and style.

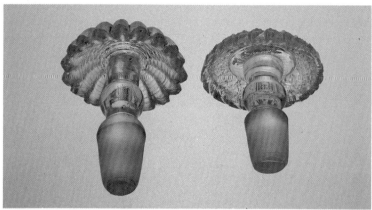

3184 PRESSED MUSHROOM DECANTER STOPPERS
(a) Ribbed 3¼" H. x 2¼" Dia. 1825–1830
(b) Lacy 2¾" H. x 2⅜" Dia. 1835–1845

Mushroom stoppers were used on early quart decanters. These two patterns are the only pressed mushroom stoppers dug at the factory site in sufficient quantity to guarantee that they were made by the Boston and Sandwich Glass Company. Cover the top half of each stopper, and you will see a simple ball stopper. The mushroom is connected to the ball by a plain shank, and the ball becomes a knop between the shank and the plug.

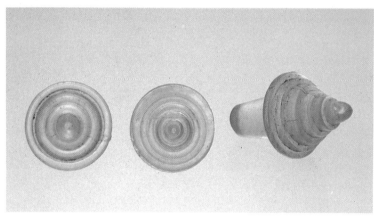

3185 PRESSED CONCENTRIC RINGED STOPPERS
(a) Three rings 1¼" H.
(b) Five rings 1⅛" H.
(c) Five stepped rings 2" H. 1828–1835

These stoppers are crude and were made very early at Sandwich. They pre-date the stopper wheel and came from a primitive mold that pressed several stoppers at a time on top of a rectangular block. This type fits loosely into its bottle in the same manner as the early Tam-o'-shanter stopper. When properly machined, the plug runs straight down from underneath the largest ring, allowing the bottom of the largest ring to rest on the rim of its bottle.

3186 HAND-FORMED FLAT-SIDED STOPPERS
1⅛" H.-2¼" H. 1825–1840

All nine of these stoppers have pontil marks on the plug end. Some were hand made in their entirety, while others were pre-shaped in a mold. All were made before the invention of the wheel mold, which was patented by Hiram Dillaway in 1841.

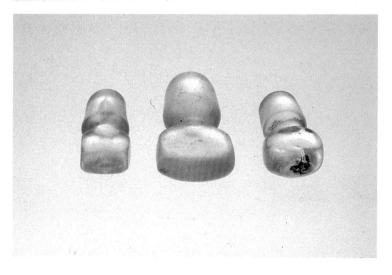

3187 HAND-FORMED FLAT-SIDED STOPPERS
(a) Finial and plug are same width 1⅛" H.
(b) Finial is wider than plug 1½" H.
(c) Incomplete finial 1⅛" H. 1825–1830

These clear glass stoppers were dug at the 1830 dump area in Sandwich. They are poor in quality and are incomplete. Stopper A has a small hole in the bottom of the plug, making it useless. Stopper B is a good example of a hand-formed flat-sided stopper. Stopper C has an incomplete finial because the glass cooled before the shaping was completed. When the glassworker attempted to reheat it, he picked up carbon by striking the stopper on the edge of the glory hole. The carbon is still embedded in the finial. We did not dig at the factory site to find perfect pieces, but to gain knowledge through the imperfect pieces discarded at the time.

3188 PRESSED FLAT-SIDED STOPPERS

(a) Square finial, long plug
(b) Rounded finial, long plug
(c) Rounded finial, short plug 1¼" H. 1830–1835
Stopper A shows the bottom of the plug not yet machined, but the side of the plug has been machined to fit a bottle. Stopper B is completely machined and is ready for use. Stopper C has a large part of the stopper block still attached. It has not been machined at all. Incomplete pieces were most important to find at the factory site, because even the most exacting critic cannot deny that they were manufactured by the Boston and Sandwich Glass Company.

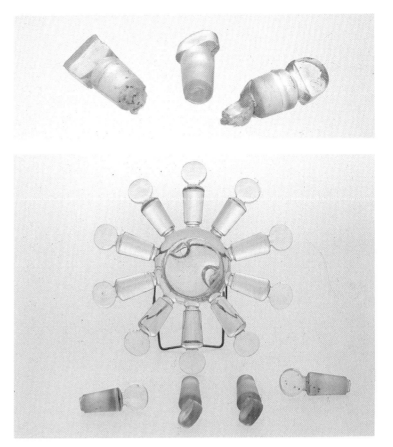

3189 WHEEL OF PRESSED FLAT-SIDED STOPPERS

2¾" H. each stopper 1841–1850
Although this method of pressing stoppers was used by many companies, the two wheels shown in this chapter are believed to be Sandwich because many matching stoppers of this type have been dug there. Keep in mind that stoppers that have been machined to fit bottles are not *proof* of production. They could have come from containers that brought material into the factory and were thrown into the dump when empty. The loose stoppers here do not show machining. Their plugs still have mold marks. They were dropped at the time the stoppers were broken away from the center fountain. When found at a glass factory site in large quantities, they can be considered part of the production run. As many as twenty-four stoppers could be pressed at one time. The discoloration on dug stoppers is caused by iron oxides in the soil.

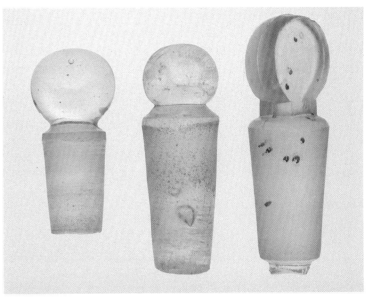

3190 FLAT-SIDED STOPPERS

(a) Hand-formed 2⅛" H.
(b) Hand-formed 2½" H. 1825–1845
(c) Pressed by wheel method 2⅞" H. 1841–1850
Note the differences between the hand-formed stoppers and the pressed stopper. The finials on stoppers A and B are rounded, as if shaped from a lump of putty. The finial on stopper C has sharp edges around the circumference and a distinct mold mark. In order to identify a possibly defective mold cavity, some stoppers from a wheel have a number *molded* into them in the center just above the plug, as appears on stopper C. Each stopper cavity had a different number. If some stoppers came out defective, the problem mold form could be identified. Do not mistake this number for a number *inscribed* on a fitted stopper that would match a number inscribed on its bottle.

3191 WHEEL OF PRESSED FLAT-SIDED STOPPERS

2⅛" H. each stopper 1841–1850
This wheel of stoppers is one of the best ever found from this time period. The amber color was common to the Keene-Stoddard area, but we do not attribute glass to a particular factory by color alone. This color matches the candlestick shown on photo 4042 of Volume 4. The candlestick has family ties to a Sandwich glassworker, and many stoppers that match in shape and color have been dug at Sandwich. Most of the dug stoppers still have a mold mark down the side of the plug, assuring us that they were manufactured by the Boston and Sandwich Glass Company.

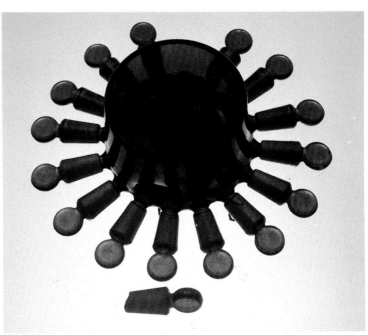

3192 PRESSED FLAT-SIDED STOPPERS
2⅛" H. 1841–1850

Hundreds of these stoppers that match the stoppers still attached to the wheel have been salvaged from the site. Most have not been machined. They were dropped at the time they were broken off the center fountain of the wheel. They ended up on the floor and were swept out with the trash to be salvaged by us 125 years later. Only the center hub of the wheel was returned to be used for cullet. Stoppers were not worth the effort.

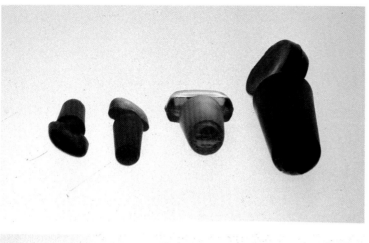

3193 PRESSED FLAT-SIDED STOPPERS
1⅜" H.–2¾" H. 1830–1835

Hundreds of these stoppers in dark "bottle" colors of amber and green have been dug at the Boston and Sandwich Glass Company site, yet few of their matching bottles or necks of bottles were found. Four sizes of stoppers are shown here, all in dark amber. They are solid glass, broken away from a stopper block. The lack of matching bottles remains an unsolved mystery of the digging site. Are they still beneath the soil, or were they returned to the cullet shop to be used in future batches? Or, were stoppers made in large quantities and sent to Deming Jarves' New England Glass Bottle Company in East Cambridge?

3194 PRESSED FLAT-SIDED PERFUME STOPPER
¾" H. 1830–1835

This stopper is compared to the size of a penny. Note the bottom of the plug where the stopper was broken off the block. When completed, this area would have been machined off, leaving a smooth area on the end where a number would be inscribed to match the number inscribed on its bottle. This tiny stopper was for a perfume used in a purse.

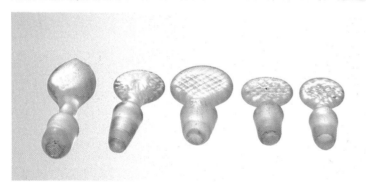

3195 HAND-FORMED SUNBURST AND WAFFLE DECANTER STOPPERS
(a) Blank
(b) Sunburst
(c, d, e) Waffle 1½" H.–2¼" H. 1825–1828

Stopper A shows the shape of the finial before the pattern was pressed into it. After reheating, the desired pattern was pressed into it by means of two patterned dies, one on each side of a pair of pincers. Stopper B has been pressed into a Sunburst pattern and stoppers C, D, and E have three variations of Waffle pattern.

3196 HAND-FORMED SUNBURST DECANTER STOPPERS
2¼" H.–3⅜" H. 1825–1835

All of the stoppers shown here were dug at the site of the Boston and Sandwich Glass Company, and each one has a different variation of the Sunburst pattern on its finial. All of the finials have one thing in common—the centers of the Sunbursts are clear. It has sometimes been claimed that the pattern on decanter stoppers can reveal which glass house in New England made them. In our opinion, this is not true. Many variations of the Sunburst were made in Sandwich, as well as at other factories.

3197 HAND-FORMED SUNBURST DECANTER STOPPERS

(a, c) Clear center
(b) Clear center, ring around edge 3" H. 1825-1835
Here are three variations of the Sunburst, all with clear centers. The same pattern is always repeated on the other side of the finial. Stopper B is considerably different from the others. There is a ring around the finial near the outer edge that cuts through the rays of the Sunburst pattern. Little or no machining was done to make the stoppers fit snugly in their decanters.

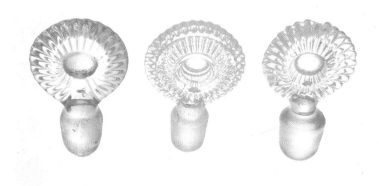

3198 HAND-FORMED SUNBURST DECANTER STOPPERS WITH TWO-RING CENTER

(a) Small finial with thick shank
(b) Large finial with thick shank
(c) Small finial with no shank 2⅜" H. 1825-1828
Two concentric rings and a protruding knob can be seen in the center of each Sunburst pattern. These stoppers should have little or no machining on the plug, because very early stoppers were made to fit loosely into their decanters. Their only purpose was to act as a cover to keep out dirt and insects.

3199 HAND-FORMED SUNBURST TOY DECANTER STOPPERS

1" H.-1½" H. 1825-1830
Toy decanters are listed in the Sandwich Glass Manufactory sloar book (also called a *turn book*) on July 9, 1825, the first full day glass was made in Sandwich. All seven stoppers shown here are a variation of the Sunburst pattern, pressed into their finials by a variety of dies on the pincers. More than sixty Sunburst toy decanter stoppers in perfect condition have been dug at the Sandwich site, in these seven Sunburst patterns.

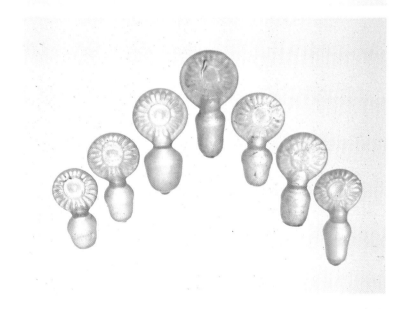

3200 HAND-FORMED SUNBURST DECANTER STOPPERS WITH WAFFLE CENTER

(a) Large plug 3¼" H.
(b) Small plug 2⅞" H. 1825-1835
The pattern on these stoppers is often thought to be solely the work of Thomas Cains, who was affiliated first with the South Boston Flint Glass Company and then with the Phoenix Glass Works, which he built across the street. We are sure Cains used this pattern, but so did Sandwich. We see no way to distinguish between them. Note the flattened edge of both finials. On stopper A, it can be seen left of the center, near the top. Stopper B is flat at the extreme right. The flat edges were made by the ends of the pincers where the dies were attached.

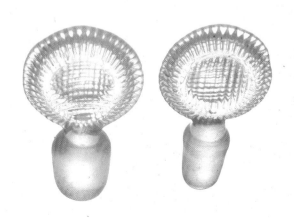

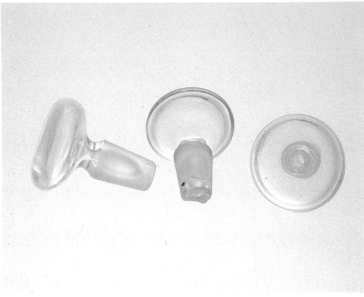

3201 BLOWN FLAT-TOPPED DECANTER STOPPERS

(a) Fitted to a decanter
(b) Dug from site
(c) Top view 2⅛" H. 1840–1860

Many stoppers blown in this shape have been dug at Sandwich, and are used on pint and half-pint decanters. The stopper on the left was taken from a known Sandwich decanter. The center stopper was dug in an area of the factory dump where known 1850–1860 debris was discarded. It matches the left stopper in every detail. The stopper on the right was also dug. This top view shows the airtrap in the finial.

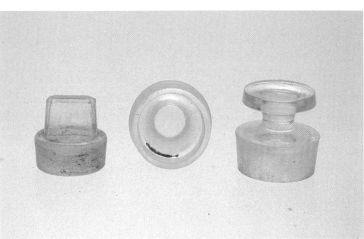

3202 BLOWN MOLDED FLAT STOPPERS

(a) Flat-sided finial 1" H. x 1⅛" Dia.
(b) Flat-topped finial, bottom view, closed across bottom of plug 1¼" H. x 1¼" Dia.
(c) Flat-topped finial 1¼" H. x 1¼" Dia. 1830–1870

Stoppers like these were used on tincture bottles and salt mouths. All those dug at the Boston and Sandwich Glass Company site have been clear, ranging in size from ¾" to 6" in diameter. They are machined to fit snugly into a jar and were often left roughly ground to increase friction. Stopper B has been positioned to show the hollow center. It is closed across the bottom, making an airtrap in the plug. Some were accidentally left open across the bottom and were discarded.

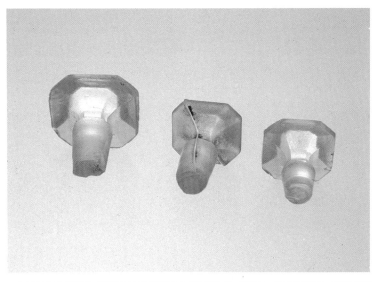

3203 PRESSED SQUARE COLOGNE STOPPERS WITH CHAMFERRED CORNERS

(a) Plug broken when machined 1⅜" H.
(b) Perfect plug ready to be machined 1¼" H.
(c) Finished and fitted to cologne 1⅛" H. 1850–1860

Here is the same type of stopper in three stages of development. Stopper A was broken when the plug was being worked on. Stopper B shows where the plug was broken away from the block or wheel fountain. The mold mark can clearly be seen running across the bottom of the finial and down the side of the plug. Stopper C is a completed perfect stopper taken from a cologne. The finial has been polished. Both the stopper and the cologne are inscribed with the number 6.

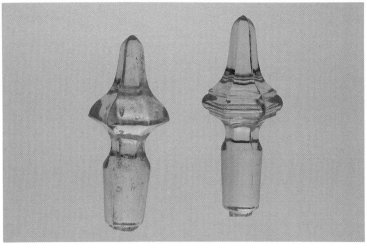

3204 PRESSED FLARING HEXAGONAL STOPPERS

(a) Plain 2¼" H. 1830–1887
(b) Detailed 2¼" H. 1840–1887

Stopper A can be found on very early cruet bottles for caster sets that pre-date revolving caster stands. It was made as small as 1¼" H. for use in toy caster sets that were made up to the time of the closing of the Boston and Sandwich Glass Company. Stopper B has a ridge above and below the widest point of the finial. It is usually found on caster sets that rotate. Both stoppers have been dug in quantity. Over two hundred are in our collection alone—some in green, canary, and dark red. In our opinion, colored caster sets were made on special order.

3205 PRESSED CRUET STOPPERS
3" H.–3¾" H. 1840–1870
Here is a group of stoppers that were used in vinegar cruets and caster bottles. They are all solid glass, so were undoubtedly pressed in stopper molds that used either the wheel configuration or a block. Although some appear to have cut facets, close examination reveals that the only finish work done was the machining of the plugs.

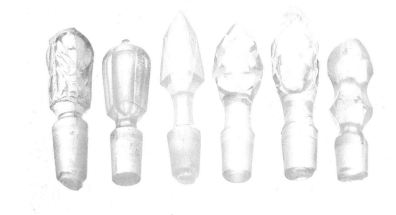

3206 BLOWN MOLDED COLOGNE STOPPERS
(a) Short stocky finial 3" H.
(b) Taller finial, blunted point 3½" H.
(c) Like B but sharp point 3⅝" H. 1840–1870
These stoppers were blown into a mold, annealed, and then six flutes were cut around the top of the finials. Note that each cutter shaped the same stopper blank differently. Stopper C is the most difficult to maintain in perfect condition. The slightest pressure against the sharp point would chip it. Learn to identify Sandwich glass by studying the shape of the blanks. The stoppers in the photo have variations in cutting, but the shape of the blanks is identical.

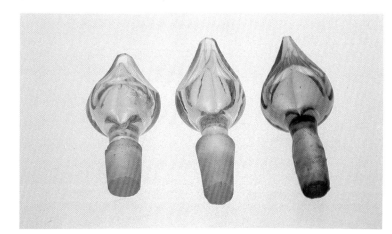

3207 COLOGNE STOPPERS
(a) Light blue, blown molded 3⅜" H. 1840–1870
(b) Dark blue, pressed 3⅝" H. 1841–1870
These stoppers are essentially the same. They were put to the same use and have the same market value. But stopper A was blown. There is an airtrap in the finial and no mold marks below the flutes, which were cut into the stopper after it was annealed. Stopper B was pressed and is the style illustrated in Hiram Dillaway's patent number 2226 that is dated August 21, 1841. There is no airtrap in the finial and a mold mark can be seen in the shank between the cut facets of the finial and the machined sides of the plug. Dillaway illustrates ten stoppers being pressed at one time using his wheel method. Blown stoppers could not be made as quickly.

3208 BLOWN MOLDED COLOGNE STOPPERS
(a) Six flutes, facets below 2¾" H. 1845–1860
(b) Eight flutes, facets below 4⅛" H. 1855–1870
Stopper A is similar in shape to the stoppers illustrated in Hiram Dillaway's patent for *pressing* many stoppers at a time, but this one is *blown* into a mold. Six flutes are cut into the pointed end of the stopper blank, with facets below. The finial was polished after the cutting was completed. Stopper B is a beautifully blown one, with eight flutes cut into it. Both stoppers were used on numerous Sandwich colognes. Although the blanks for both stoppers are similar in shape, the cutting changed the contour.

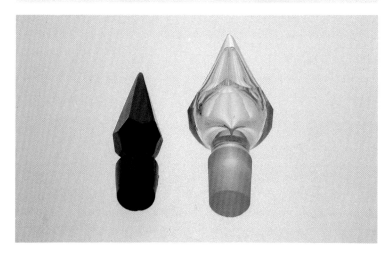

3209 PRESSED GILDED STOPPERS
(a) Light blue 2¼" H.
(b) Clear 2¼" H.
(c) Blue 2½" H.
(d) Dark green 2½" H. 1845–1860

Based on shape and color, these stoppers could have been made as early as 1840. But the man called "William Smith, the gilder" did not come to the Boston and Sandwich Glass Company until the mid-1840's to head the company's new decorating shop. The gilding can best be seen on stopper C, a large dot on each of the panels. A gold dot is also applied on the very top of the finial. None of these stoppers have been machined to fit a bottle. Stopper B shows the mold mark running down the side of the plug just left of center.

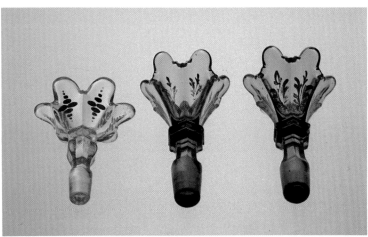

3210 PRESSED GILDED COLOGNE STOPPERS
(a) Flower 2½" H. x 2¼" Dia.
(b, c) Lily 3¾" H. x 2" Dia. 1845–1870

Stopper A has a protuberance below the petals much like a real flower. Sometimes the petals were reworked to flare out, or close up into a bud. The Lily stoppers have two hexagonal rings below and are the trumpet shape of a real lily. Note the gilding on all three stoppers. The light, sandy soil of Sandwich has preserved the decorations so that rubbing with toothpaste on a soft cloth, even after one hundred years in the ground, restored the gilding perfectly.

3211 PRESSED FLOWER COLOGNE STOPPERS
(a) Large 3" H. x 3" Dia.
(b) Medium 2½" H. x 2¾" Dia.
(c) Small 2¼" H. x 2½" Dia. 1840–1870

Flower stoppers are beautifully made and add a special quality to the cologne. Stopper A fits a cologne that holds one quart and has an underplate. Stopper B was used on a one pint cologne and stopper C on a half pint bottle. No other American glass factory made a stopper that is even close to this configuration, but a similar one was made in France. It has not been reproduced.

3212 CUT OVERLAY COLOGNE STOPPERS
(a) Green, plug not machined 3¾" H.
(b) Blue, plug partly machined 3½" H.
(c) Blue, ready for use 2⅜" H. 1845–1870

Overlay is glass cased on the outside with one or two different colors. The outer layer (or layers) are cut back to reveal the glass beneath. When stopper A was blown, the layer of green was carried down over the plug. The stopper was never fitted to a bottle, so the green remains. Stopper B has the blue overlay removed. Two other identical stoppers were dug at the same time along with the bottle shown in photo 3137 in the chapter on colognes. Stopper C was ready to be inserted into a cologne bottle. It is inscribed with a number and is in perfect condition. There was no reason to discard it, unless its matching bottle was damaged and discarded.

3213 PRESSED FACETED STOPPERS
(a) Amber, machined plug 2½" H.
(b) Light canary, machined plug 2½" H.
(c) Light amethyst, machined plug 3" H.
(d) Light blue, plug not machined 3¼" H. 1870–1887

Three types of faceted stoppers were made in Sandwich: pressed faceted, pressed lapidary, and blown molded lapidary. *Pressed* faceted stoppers were formed in a mold that had the pattern of facets in it. The only work that had to be done after it was removed from the faceted mold and annealed was machining the plug. They had the least clarity and were the least expensive. All of the stoppers shown here were pressed by the wheel method. Each is from a different mold, but the same number of facets are pressed into each finial. Stopper D was not machined. The mold mark can be seen running down the side of the plug.

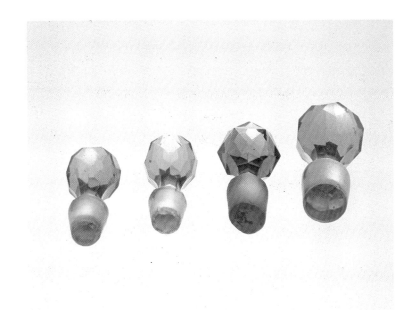

3214 PRESSED FACETED STOPPERS
(a) Light amber, machined plug
(b) Amber, plug not machined 3" H. 1860–1887

Stopper A is a finished stopper. It was machined to fit a bottle, and a number is inscribed on the bottom of the plug. The same number would have been inscribed on the bottle to which the stopper was fitted. We cannot be absolutely sure that this stopper was made by the Boston and Sandwich Glass Company even though it was dug there, unless additional identical stoppers are found that still show the mold mark. The stopper could have been on a bottle that was brought to the factory by a worker who purchased it elsewhere. When the bottle was empty, it could have been thrown in the dump, and therefore historians should not attribute it to Sandwich. Stopper B was made at Sandwich. Note the mold mark on the plug. It was dropped when the cutter was shaping the end of the plug.

3215 PRESSED LAPIDARY STOPPERS
(a) Polished finial, machined plug 3" H.
(b) Unpolished finial, machined plug 3" H.
(c) Polished finial, cut hexagonal shank, partly
    machined plug 4¾" H. 1870–1887

A second type of faceted stopper is the pressed lapidary stopper made by *polishing* the facets of a pressed faceted stopper. This extra step resulted in added clarity. All three stoppers shown here were intended to have their facets polished. Stopper A is complete except for the missing inscribed number. Stopper B has a machined plug, but the first attempt to polish the facets chipped it. As the plug on stopper C was machined, it went out of round and was rendered useless. Note that stoppers A and B have no shank. Stopper C has a long shank, cut into six sides to enhance its beauty. There could be as many as fifty-two facets on each finial.

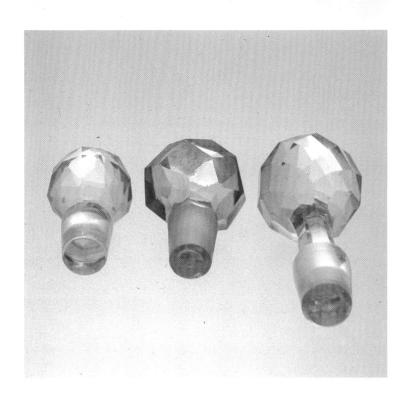

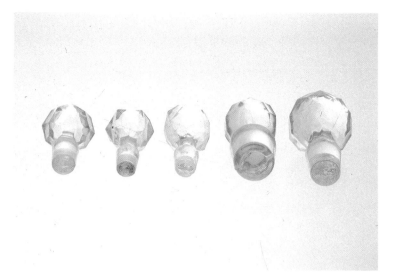

3216 PRESSED LAPIDARY STOPPERS
2¼" H.-3" H. 1870–1887

These stoppers were pressed on a stopper wheel; there are no airtraps in their centers. Note the variations in the size of the plugs, which extend from the finials with no shank between. The facets of all five stoppers were polished after they were removed from the wheel and annealed. They were considered excellent substitutes for blown lapidary stoppers.

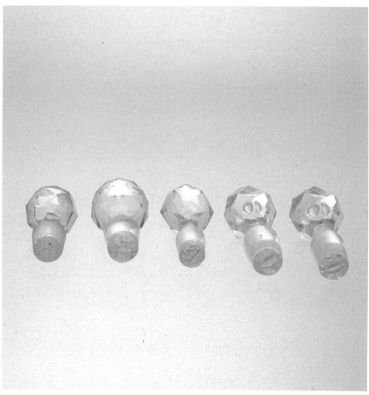

3217 LAPIDARY STOPPERS
(a, b, c) Pressed, no airtrap
(d, e) Blown molded, with airtrap 2¼" H.-2¾" H.
      1870–1887

A third type of faceted stopper was made by blowing glass into a mold that had the pattern of facets in it. Stoppers D and E were made in this manner. Note the airtrap in their centers. If they were pressed, they would be solid, as are stoppers A, B, and C. Blown faceted stoppers have greater brilliance than pressed faceted stoppers. They were made from the highest quality glass and reached their zenith during what is known as the *Brilliant Period* in cut glass manufacture. They represent some of the finest faceting executed in Sandwich.

3218 BLOWN MOLDED STOPPERS FOR LATE BLOWN WARE
(a) Curtain design, copper wheel engraved on finial, six flutes cut into shank 4¼" H.
(b) Fern design, copper wheel engraved on finial, plain shank 4¼" H.
(c) Copper wheel engraved design and cut star on finial, long shank with faceted knop center 4½" H.
(d) Cut star on finial with cut flutes below, and airtrap extending into plug 1870–1887

The Late Blown Period in the history of the Boston and Sandwich Glass Company coincided with the Brilliant Period in cut glass manufacture. The finials were blown "thin as a bubble". Note the airtrap that extends into the plug of stopper D. The plug of stopper B was damaged when it was machined.

3219 BLOWN MOLDED STOPPERS

(a) Bands of ribbing and diamond diapering 3½" H. 1830
(b) Diamond Thumbprint pattern 3¾" H. 1840
(c) Threaded glass 2½" H. 1880
(d) Late blown ware, Etched 500 design 4" H. 1885

Compare stopper A with stopper D, and note the improvement in workmanship. Note also the evolution of the plug, from a loosely fitting one that only protected the contents of the bottle from dirt and insects, to a sophisticated plug individually fitted to one particular bottle, preventing evaporation of its contents. The patterns on stoppers A and B were completed simply by blowing the glass into patterned molds. The threading on stopper C was applied after the stopper was removed from an unpatterned mold, then the stopper was annealed. Stopper D was blown into an unpatterned mold, annealed, then the design was etched into its surface.

3220 PRESSED FLAT-SIDED WHISKEY JUG STOPPERS

(a, c) Lacy Teardrop design copper wheel engraved on finial
(b) Blank 2¾" H. 1870–1887

The decanters to which these stoppers were fitted were the short, squat, handled ones listed as *whiskey jugs* in the 1874 catalog of the Boston and Sandwich Glass Company. They can be seen on page 14 of the catalog reprint. Any of the Late Blown Period designs could be copper wheel engraved on the stopper blank, or have just a simple letter that indicated the contents of the jug. The letter "B" stands for brandy, and "W" denotes whiskey—they are *not* someone's monogram!

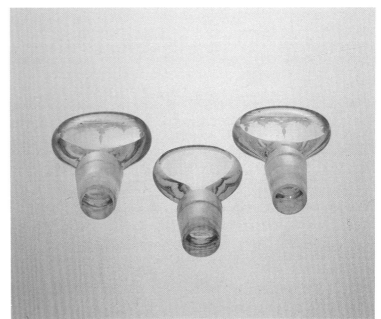

3221 BLOWN MOLDED THREADED STOPPERS

(a) Small finial, long hexagonal shank 3¾" H.
(b) Large finial, shorter plain shank 3¾" H.
(c) Short plain shank 2¾" H.
(d) Short plain shank 2¼" H. 1880–1887

The Late Blown Period provided some of the most beautiful glass. Although large quantities of cologne fragments were dug that have blue, green, and canary threading, all of the stoppers we found have pink threading. Out of the dozens with pink threading, only these four have perfect threads. The shank of stopper A was cut into six panels and polished. One hundred years in the soil made the threads *sick*—discolored to a pale pink. All of the threaded stoppers dug at Sandwich have threading completely covering the finials. If you buy a partly threaded stopper, it may be English.

3222 SLIDE STOPPERS
(a) Permanent cage 1¾" H. from finial to bar lip
(b) Threaded removable cage 2" H. from finial to bar lip 1850–1870

Pressed decanters were made in two styles. *Table* decanters were fitted with "glass stops", and *bar* decanters were shipped with "slide stops". To date, the four slide stoppers shown here are the only types that have been dug at the factory site. The opening in the pewter stopper that allowed the liquid to be poured out of the decanter was made in three sizes, requiring three different size marbles. The marble was inserted in a cage-like device that was permanently attached to the stopper as in A, or threaded to the stopper as in B. When the decanter was in an upright position, the marble closed the opening. When the decanter was tilted for pouring, the marble slid toward the top of the cage.

3223 SLIDE STOPPERS
(a) Wire cage 2" H. from top of cage to bar lip
(b) Permanent cage 1⅞" H. from finial to bar lip 1850–1870

Slide stoppers with wire cages are not plentiful, so they command a higher price in the antiques market. The cage of stopper B is permanently attached, but the finial is not the same as those shown in the previous photo. All four types use cork to keep them in place. The glass marbles were not made in Sandwich. Records show that the Boston and Sandwich Glass Company purchased them from German glass houses in four hundred pound casks with a guarantee that 70 percent would be usable. Glassmakers sometimes made marbles for the boys who worked at the factory or for their own children, but marbles were not manufactured for commercial purposes.

3224 SLIDE STOPPER FRAGMENTS
1850–1870

Although time has eaten away the pewter slide stoppers dug at the factory site, there is in this photo enough information to tell us what types were used and how they were assembled. The stopper at the top took the largest marble and was used on a quart decanter. The stopper below it, in the center, took the smallest marble and was used on a half pint decanter. The other three were used on pint bar decanters and utilized a medium size marble. A "slide stop" was shipped with every bar decanter, so your decanter is not complete without this upper unit.

GLOSSARY

ADVENTURINE See *goldstone*.

ANNEAL The gradual reheating and slow cooling of an article in a leer—an oven built for the purpose. This procedure removes any stress that may have built up in the glass during its manufacture.

APPLIED The fastening of a separate piece of glass, such as a base, handle, prunt, or stem, to an article already formed.

BATCH Mixture of sand, cullet, and various raw materials that are placed in the pot to be heated into metal, or molten glass.

BLANK A finished piece of glass requiring additional work, such as decorating or engraving.

BLOWN GLASS Glass made by the use of a blowpipe and air pressure sufficient to give it form.

BLOWN MOLDED GLASS Glass made by blowing hot glass into a plain or patterned mold, and forcing it with air pressure to conform to the shape of the mold.

BOX A container of any shape and any size. It can be square, rectangular, circular or oval.

BUTTON STEM A connector between the base and the body of any article, with a button-shaped extrusion in its center.

CANE In *paperweight making*, a bundle of various colored rods that are arranged into a design, fused by reheating, pulled until it is long and thin, cooled and then cut into segments.

CASING A different colored layer of glass, either on the inside or outside of the main body of a piece.

CASTOR PLACE The location in the factory where glass was cast (pressed) into molds.

CLAW FOOT An applied reeded foot resembling a scallop shell.

CLUSTER On *cut glass*, a grouping of similar designs in close proximity.

CRAQUELLE Glass that has been deliberately fractured after it has been formed, and reheated to seal the fractures, leaving the scars as a permanent design.

CROSSCUT DIAMOND On *cut glass*, a diamond that is divided into quarters.

CULLET Glass made in the factory and saved from a pot to be used in making future batches. Also, glass items already annealed; either produced in the factory or purchased, and broken to be included in future batches.

CUTTING The grinding away of a portion of the surface of a blank, using wheels and wet sand, to produce a design.

DECORATING The ornamenting of a blank by painting or staining it with a non-glass substance.

DESIGN The ornamentation of glass after it has been annealed, by cutting, engraving, etching or decorating.

DONUT On *Trevaise*, the wafer-size glob of glass applied to the base. In most cases, the center of the wafer is dished out, leaving the shape of a donut.

ENGRAVING The process of cutting shallow designs and letters into a blank using copper wheels and an abrasive.

ETCHING An inexpensive method of producing a design by using hydrofluoric acid to eat into the surface of a blank.

FILIGREE ROD A rod that has spiral or straight threads running through it. Also called *latticinio*.

FINIAL The decorative, terminal part of a newel post, writing pen, etc. The part of a cover used as a handle.

FIRE POLISHING Reheating a finished piece to remove marks left by tools or molds, leaving the article with a smooth surface.

FLASHED On *cut glass*, a fan-like design located between the points of a fan, hobstar, or star.

FLINT GLASS Glass made from metal containing lead. In the 1800's, the factory term for clear glass.

FLOATED In *decorated opal glass*, the method used to apply a solid color background.

FLUTE The hand-crimping of a rim. On *pressed* or *cut glass*, a panel rounded at the top.

FOLDED RIM A rim on either the body or base of a piece, the edge of which is doubled back onto itself, resulting in greater strength.

FRAGMENTS Broken pieces of finished glass, discarded at the time of production.

FREE-BLOWN GLASS Glass made by blowing hot glass and shaping it into its final form by the use of hand tools.

GAFFER In a group of glassworkers, called a *shop*, the most skilled artisan; the master glass blower.

GATHER The mass of hot metal that has been gathered on the end of a blowpipe.

GATHERER The assistant to the master glass blower, who gathers the hot metal on the end of the blowpipe.

GAUFFER To crimp or flute.

GILDING The application of gold for decorative purposes.

GLASS GALL Impurities skimmed from the surface of melted glass. Also called *sandever, sandiver*.

GOLDSTONE Glass combined with copper filings.

HOBSTAR On *cut glass*, a many-pointed geometrically cut star.

KNOP A round knob, either hollow or solid, in the center of a stem.

LAMPWORK The making and assembly of leaves, petals, stems, fruit and other small parts from rods of glass that have been softened by heating them over a gas burner. Originally, oil lamps produced the open flame.

LAPIDARY STOPPER A cut, faceted stopper.

LATTICINIO A rod of glass or a paperweight background composed of threads arranged in lattice, spiral or swirl configurations. The threads are usually white.

LEER A tunnel-shaped oven through which glass articles are drawn after formation for the purpose of annealing. Also spelled *lear, lehr*.

MAKE-DO A damaged item that has been repaired to "make it do" what was originally intended.

MARBRIE In *blown glass*, a loop design made by looping and trailing threads of glass through another color, such as in paperweights and witch balls.

MARVER Iron plate on which hot glass is first shaped by rolling, in preparation for blowing into its final form.

MERESE A wafer-shaped piece of hot glass, used to connect individual units to make a complete piece, such as the base and socket of a candlestick or the bowl and standard of a footed nappie.

METAL Glass either in a molten condition in the pot, or in a cold, hardened state.

MOLD A form into which glass is blown or pressed to give it shape and pattern. Also spelled *mould*.

MOLD MARKS On glass that has been blown or pressed into a mold, the marks or seam lines left by the edges of the units of the mold.

MOVE A period of time during which a shop makes glass continuously. A glass blower is expected to make ten *moves* each week.

NAPPIE A shallow bowl of any size, whether round bottomed or flat bottomed, which can be on a standard. Also spelled *nappy*.

NEEDLE ETCHING Done by coating a blank with an acid-resisting substance, then inscribing a design into the resist with a sharp needle. The blank is then dipped into hydrofluoric acid, which etches the glass where the design was inscribed.

NIB The writing point of a pen.

OVERFILL On pieces that have been blown or pressed into a mold, the excess hot glass that seeps into the seams of the mold.

PANEL A section with raised margins and square corners.

PATTERN (ON GLASS) The specific ornamentation into which *hot* glass is formed.

PATTERN (WOODEN) Wooden model carved in detail that is sent to the foundry, used as a guide to shape a mold.

PEG On a *lamp*, the unit that holds the oil and is attached to the base with a metal connector.

PICKWICK A pointed instrument for picking up the wick of a whale oil or fluid lamp.

PILLAR-MOLDED GLASS Glass made by first blowing a hot gather of glass into a mold with vertical ridges (pillars). A second cooler gather is blown into the first. The hot outer layer conforms to the shape of the mold, while the cooler inner layer remains smooth.

PINWHEEL On *cut glass*, a design resembling a hobstar in motion; its points angled in a clockwise or counter-clockwise position.

PONTIL MARK Rough spot caused by breaking away the pontil rod.

PONTIL ROD A rod or iron used by glassworkers to hold the glass while it is being formed.

POT A one-piece container in which glass is melted, usually made of clay and able to withstand extreme heat.

PLINTH A square block forming the base for a standard. Also, a base and standard molded in one piece, used as the lower unit of a lamp.

PRESSED GLASS Glass made by placing hot glass into a mold and forcing it with a plunger to conform to the shape of the mold.

PRISM A pattern or design of deep parallel V-grooves that reflect the light.

PRUNT A blob of glass applied to the surface of a vessel, for the purpose of decorating or hiding a defect.

PUNTING The process of dishing out a circle with a cutting wheel, usually to remove the mark left by the pontil rod.

PUNTY A concave circle made by dishing out the glass with a cutting wheel.

QUILTING In *art glass*, an all-over diamond design, permanently molded into the piece as it was being blown.

RIBBON ROD A rod that has twisted flat ribbons of glass running through it.

RIGAREE A heavy thread of glass applied to the surface of a piece, giving a decorative rippled or fluted effect.

ROD A straight shaft of glass that will be reheated to form other things. Thin rods are fused together to make canes, and are also softened to supply glass for lampwork. Thick rods are formed into chandelier arms and epergne units. Reeded rods are used to form handles and claw feet on Late Blown Ware, as well as nibs for glass writing pens.

SERVITOR The first assistant to the gaffer in a group of glassworkers called a *shop*.

SHEDDING The flaking of the surface of finished glass exposed to the air, cause by minute particles of fire clay in the sand. According to C. C. P. Waterman, writing in 1875, " . . . small specks of fire clay which shed themselves very much to their annoyance throughout the melted glass."

SHELL FOOT See *claw foot*.

SHOP A group of workmen producing glass at the furnace, consisting of a master glass blower and his help.

SICK GLASS Discoloration of the surface of an article.

SLOAR BOOK The book in which an accounting was kept of the output of glass produced by each shop at the furnace.

SLOAR MAN The glassworker who entered the output of each shop in the sloar book.

SOCKET EXTENSION On a *candlestick*, the section between the socket and the wafer, molded in one piece with the socket.

SPIDER PONTIL An iron unit placed on the end of the pontil rod, consisting of several finger-like rods. The fingers gave support to items that could not be held by a single rod in the center.

STAINED GLASS A finished piece of clear glass that is colored wholly or in part by the application of a chemical dye—most commonly ruby. The article is re-fired, making the dye a permanent finish.

STICKER-UP BOY The boy who carries hot glass on a V-shaped stick in a group of glassworkers called a *shop*.

STRAWBERRY DIAMOND On *cut glass*, a diamond which is crosshatched. Also the name of a cut glass design that utilizes crosscut diamonds.

TAKER-IN BOY The boy who carries the hot finished product to the leer in a group of glassworkers called a *shop*. During slow periods, he assists in the removal of glass from the cold end of the leer.

TALE Articles sold by count rather than by weight. In the words of Deming Jarves, "Tale was derived from the mode of selling, the best glass being sold only by weight, while light articles were sold tale."

UNDERFILL An insufficient amount of glass blown or pressed into a mold, resulting in an incomplete product. This is a characteristic, not a defect.

VESICA On *cut glass*, a pointed oval.

WAFER A flattened piece of hot glass, sometimes called a merese, used to join separately made units into a complete piece, such as the base and socket of a candlestick or the bowl and standard of a footed nappie.

WHIMSEY Unusual, one-of-a-kind item made of glass by a worker in his spare time.

INVENTORY OF SANDWICH GLASS

No.	Description	Condition	Date Purchased	Amount	Date Sold	Amount

BIBLIOGRAPHY

UNPUBLISHED SOURCES

Account book of various activities of the Boston and Sandwich Glass Company, such as the company store, sea-going vessels, wages, and wood for construction and fuel. April 17, 1826, to July 1830. Ms. collection in the Tannahill Research Library, Henry Ford Museum, Edison Institute, Dearborn, Michigan.

Burbank, George E. *History of the Sandwich Glass Works.* Ms. in the Barlow collection.

Corporate records. Office of the Secretary of State, The Commonwealth of Massachusetts, Boston, Massachusetts.

Correspondence pertaining to the management of the Boston and Sandwich Glass Company and the Cape Cod Glass Company, such as glass formulas, letters, special notices and transfers. Ms. collection in the Tannahill Research Library, Henry Ford Museum, Edison Institute, Dearborn, Michigan.

Correspondence pertaining to the management of the Boston and Sandwich Glass Company, the Boston and Sandwich Glass Company II and the Cape Cod Glass Company, such as glass formulas, letters, statements, etc. Ms. collection in the Rakow Library, The Corning Museum of Glass, Corning, New York.

Correspondence to and from glass authorities and writers on the subject of glass, pertaining to the excavation of the Boston and Sandwich Glass Company site and the discussion of fragments. Ms. consisting of the Francis (Bill) Wynn papers, now in the Barlow collection.

Documentation in the form of fragments dug from factory and cutting shop sites. Private collections and the extensive Barlow collection, which includes the former Francis (Bill) Wynn collection.

Documentation of Sandwich glass items and Sandwich glassworkers, such as hand-written notebooks, letters, billheads, contracts, pictures, and oral history of Sandwich families recorded on tape by descendants. Ms. in the Barlow collection, Kaiser collection and private collections.

Documents pertaining to the genealogy of the family of Deming Jarves. Mount Auburn Cemetery, Cambridge, Massachusetts.

Documents pertaining to the Sandwich glass industry and other related industries, such as statistics from Sandwich Vital Records, information from property tax records, maps, photographs, family papers and genealogy. Ms. in the care of the Town of Sandwich Massachusetts Archives and Historical Center, Sandwich, Massachusetts.

Documents relating to the North Sandwich industrial area, such as photographs, account books and handwritten scrapbooks. Ms. in the private collection of Mrs. Edward "Ned" Nickerson and the Bourne Historical Society, Bourne, Massachusetts.

Documents relating to the Sandwich Co-operative Glass Company, such as account books, correspondence and glass formulas. Ms. in the private collection of Murray family descendants.

Glass formula book. "Sandwich Aug. 7, 1868, James D. Lloyd." Ms. collection in the Tannahill Research Library, Henry Ford Museum, Edison Institute, Dearborn, Michigan.

Lapham family documents, such as pictures and genealogy. Ms. in the private collections of Lapham family descendants.

Lutz family documents, such as pictures, handwritten biographies and genealogy. Ms. in the private collections of Lutz family descendants.

Mary Gregory documents, such as diaries, letters and pictures. Ms. in the Barlow collection, Kaiser collection, other private collections, and included in the private papers of her family.

Minutes of annual meetings, Board of Directors meetings, special meetings and stockholders meetings of the Boston and Sandwich Glass Company. Ms. collection in the Tannahill Research Library, Henry Ford Museum, Edison Institute, Dearborn, Michigan.

Minutes of meetings of the American Flint Glass Workers Union, Local No. 16. Ms. in the Sandwich Glass Museum, Sandwich Historical Society, Sandwich, Massachusetts.

Nye family documents relating to the North Sandwich industrial area and the Electrical Glass Corporation. Ms. in the Barlow-Kaiser collection.

Oral history recorded on tape. Tales of Cape Cod, Inc. collection in the Cape Cod Community College Library, Hyannis, Massachusetts.

Patents relating to the invention of new techniques in glassmaking, improved equipment for glassmaking, new designs and styles of glass, and the invention of other items relating to the glass industry. United States Department of Commerce, Patent and Trademark Office, Washington, D. C.

Population Schedule of the Census of the United States. Ms. from National Archives Microfilm Publications, National Archives and Records Service, Washington, D. C.

Property deeds and other proofs of ownership, such as surveys, mortagage deeds, and last will and testaments. Ms. in the Barnstable County Registry of Deeds and Barnstable County Registry of Probate, Barnstable, Massachusetts.

Sloar book, a weekly accounting of glass produced at the Sandwich Glass Manufactory and the Boston and Sandwich Glass Company, and the workers who produced it. July 9, 1825, to March 29, 1828. Ms. collection in the Tannahill Research Library, Henry Ford Museum, Edison Institute, Dearborn, Michigan.

Spurr family documents, such as pictures, handwritten autobiographies, glass formulas and genealogy. Ms. in the private collections of Spurr family descendants.

Vodon family documents, such as pictures and genealogy. Ms. in the private collection of Vodon family descendants.

Waterman, Charles Cotesworth Pinckney. Notes on the Boston and Sandwich Glass Company, dated November 1876, and deposited in the Sandwich Centennial Box. Ms. in the care of the Town of Sandwich Massachusetts Archives and Historical Center, Sandwich, Massachusetts.

PRINTED SOURCES

Amic, Yolande. *L'Opaline Francaise au XIXe Siecle*. Paris, France: Library Gründ, 1952.

Anthony, T. Robert. *19th Century Fairy Lamps*. Manchester, Vermont: Forward's Color Productions, Inc., 1969.

Avila, George C. *The Pairpoint Glass Story*. New Bedford, Massachusetts: Reynolds-DeWalt Printing, Inc., 1968.

Barbour, Harriot Buxton. *Sandwich The Town That Glass Built*. Boston, Massachusetts: Houghton Mifflin Company, 1948.

Barret, Richard Carter. *A Collectors Handbook of American Art Glass*. Manchester, Vermont: Forward's Color Productions, Inc., 1971.

_____. *A Collectors Handbook of Blown and Pressed American Glass*. Manchester, Vermont: Forward's Color Productions, Inc., 1971.

_____. *Popular American Ruby-Stained Pattern Glass*. Manchester, Vermont: Forward's Color Productions, Inc., 1968.

Belknap, E. McCamly. *Milk Glass*. New York, New York: Crown Publishers, Inc., 1949.

Bishop, Barbara. "Deming Jarves and His Glass Factories," *The Glass Club Bulletin*, Spring 1983, pp. 3-5.

Bishop, Barbara and Martha Hassell. *Your Obd^t. Servt., Deming Jarves*. Sandwich, Massachusetts: The Sand-

wich Historical Society, 1984.

Brown, Clark W. *Salt Dishes*. Leon, Iowa: Mid-America Book Company, reprinted in 1968.

_____. *A Supplement to Salt Dishes*. Leon, Iowa: Prairie Winds Press, reprinted in 1970.

Burbank, George E. *A Bit of Sandwich History*. Sandwich, Massachusetts: 1939.

Burgess, Bangs. *History of Sandwich Glass*. Yarmouth, Massachusetts: The Register Press, 1925.

Butterfield, Oliver. "Bewitching Witchballs," *Yankee*, July 1978, pp. 97, 172-175.

Cataldo, Louis and Dorothy Worrell. *Pictorial Tales of Cape Cod*. (Vol. I) Hyannis, Massachusetts: Tales of Cape Cod, Inc., 1956.

Cataldo, Louis and Dorothy Worrell. *Pictorial Tales of Cape Cod*. (Vol. II) Hyannis, Massachusetts: Tales of Cape Cod, Inc., 1961.

Childs, David B. "If It's Threaded . . . ," *Yankee*, June 1960, pp. 86-89.

Chipman, Frank W. *The Romance of Old Sandwich Glass*. Sandwich, Massachusetts: Sandwich Publishing Company Inc., 1932.

Cloak, Evelyn Campbell. *Glass Paperweights of the Bergstrom Art Center*. New York, New York: Crown Publishers, Inc., 1969.

Covill, William E., Jr. *Ink Bottles and Inkwells*. Taunton, Massachusetts: William S. Sullwold Publishing, 1971.

Culver, Willard R. "From Sand to Seer and Servant of Man," *The National Geographic Magazine*, January 1943, pp. 17-24, 41-48.

Deyo, Simeon L. *History of Barnstable County, Massachusetts*. New York, New York: H. W. Blake & Co., 1890.

DiBartolomeo, Robert E. *American Glass from the Pages of Antiques; Pressed and Cut*. (Vol. II) Princeton, New Jersey: The Pyne Press, 1974.

Dooley, William Germain. *Old Sandwich Glass*. Pasadena, California: Esto Publishing Company, n.d.

_____. "Recollections of Sandwich Glass by a Veteran Who Worked on It," *Hobbies*, June 1951, p. 96.

Drepperd, Carl W. *The ABC's of Old Glass*. Garden City, New York: Doubleday & Company, Inc., 1949.

Fauster, Carl U. *Libbey Glass Since 1818*. Toledo, Ohio: Len Beach Press, 1979.

Freeman, Frederick. *History of Cape Cod: Annals of the Thirteen Towns of Barnstable County*. Boston, Massachusetts: George C. Rand & Avery, 1862.

Freeman, Dr. Larry. *New Light on Old Lamps*. Watkins Glen, New York: American Life Foundation, reprinted in 1984.

Gaines, Edith. "Woman's Day Dictionary of American Glass," *Woman's Day*, August 1961, pp. 19-34.

_____. "Woman's Day Dictionary of Sandwich Glass," *Woman's Day*, August 1963, pp. 21-32.

_____. "Woman's Day Dictionary of Victorian Glass," *Woman's Day*, August 1964, pp. 23-34.

Gores, Stan. *1876 Centennial Collectibles and Price Guide*. Fond du Lac, Wisconsin: The Haber Printing Co., 1974.

Grover, Ray and Lee Grover. *Art Glass Nouveau*. Rutland, Vermont: Charles E. Tuttle Company, Inc., 1967.

Grover, Ray and Lee Grover. *Carved & Decorated European Art Glass*. Rutland, Vermont: Charles E. Tuttle Company, Inc., 1970.

Grow, Lawrence. *The Warner Collector's Guide to Pressed Glass*. New York, New York: Warner Books, Inc., 1982.

Hammond, Dorothy. *Confusing Collectibles*. Des Moines, Iowa: Wallace-Homestead Book Company, 1969.

_____. *More Confusing Collectibles*. Wichita, Kansas: C. B. P. Publishing Company, 1972.

Harris, Amanda B. "Down in Sandwich Town," *Wide Awake* 1, 1887, pp. 19–27.

Harris, John. *The Great Boston Fire, 1872*. Boston, Massachusetts: Boston Globe, 1972.

Hartung, Marion T. and Ione E. Hinshaw. *Patterns and Pinafores*. Des Moines, Iowa: Wallace-Homestead Book Company, 1971.

Haynes, E. Barrington. *Glass Through the Ages*. Baltimore, Maryland: Penguin Books, 1969.

Hayward, Arthur H. *Colonial and Early American Lighting*. New York, New York: Dover Publications, Inc., reprinted in 1962.

Heacock, William. *Encyclopedia of Victorian Colored Pattern Glass; Book 1 Toothpick Holders from A to Z*. Jonesville, Michigan: Antique Publications, 1974.

_____. *Encyclopedia of Victorian Colored Pattern Glass; Book 2 Opalescent Glass from A to Z*. Jonesville, Michigan: Antique Publications, 1975.

_____. *Encyclopedia of Victorian Colored Pattern Glass; Book 3 Syrups, Sugar Shakers & Cruets from A to Z*. Jonesville, Michigan: Antique Publications, 1976.

_____. *Encyclopedia of Victorian Colored Pattern Glass; Book 4 Custard Glass from A to Z*. Marietta, Ohio: Antique Publications, 1976.

_____. *Encyclopedia of Victorian Colored Pattern Glass; Book 5 U. S. Glass from A to Z*. Marietta, Ohio: Antique Publications, 1978.

_____. *Encyclopedia of Victorian Colored Pattern Glass; Book 6 Oil Cruets from A to Z*. Marietta, Ohio: Antique Publications, 1981.

_____. *1000 Toothpick Holders; A Collector's Guide*. Marietta, Ohio: Antique Publications, 1977.

Heacock, William and Patricia Johnson. *5000 Open Salts; A Collector's Guide*. Marietta, Ohio: Richardson Printing Corporation, 1982.

Heckler, Norman. *American Bottles in the Charles B. Gardner Collection*. Bolton, Massachusetts: Robert W. Skinner, Inc., 1975.

Hildebrand, J. R. "Glass Goes To Town," *The National Geographic Magazine*, January 1943, pp. 1–16, 25–40.

Hollister, Paul, Jr. *The Encyclopedia of Glass Paperweights*. New York, New York: Clarkson N. Potter, Inc., 1969.

Ingold, Gérard. *The Art of the Paperweight; Saint Louis*. Santa Cruz, California: Paperweight Press, 1981.

Innes, Lowell. *Pittsburgh Glass 1797–1891*. Boston, Massachusetts: Houghton Mifflin Company, 1976.

Irwin, Frederick T. *The Story of Sandwich Glass*. Manchester, New Hampshire: Granite State Press, 1926.

Jarves, Deming. *Reminiscences of Glass-making*. Great Neck, New York: Beatrice C. Weinstock, reprinted in 1968.

Kamm, Minnie W. and Serry Wood. *The Kamm-Wood Encyclopedia of Pattern Glass*. (II vols.) Watkins Glen, New York: Century House, 1961.

Keene, Betsey D. *History of Bourne 1622–1937*. Yarmouthport, Massachusetts: Charles W. Swift, 1937.

Knittle, Rhea Mansfield. *Early American Glass*. New York, New York: The Century Co., 1927.

Lane, Lyman and Sally Lane, and Joan Pappas. *A Rare Collection of Keene & Stoddard Glass*. Manchester, Vermont: Forward's Color Productions, Inc., 1970.

Lanmon, Dwight P. "Russian Paperweights and Letter Seals?" *The Magazine Antiques*, October 1984, pp. 900–903.

_____. "Unmasking an American Glass Fraud," *The Magazine Antiques*, January 1983, pp. 226–236.

Lechler, Doris Anderson. *Children's Glass Dishes, China, and Furniture*. Paducah, Kentucky: Collector Books, 1983.

Lechler, Doris and Virginia O'Neill. *Children's Glass Dishes*. Nashville, Tennessee, 1976.

Lee, Ruth Webb. *Antique Fakes & Reproductions*. Wellesley Hills, Massachusetts: Lee Publications, 1966.

_____. *Early American Pressed Glass*. Wellesley Hills, Massachusetts: Lee Publications, 1960.

_____. *Nineteenth-Century Art Glass*. New York, New York: M. Barrows & Company, Inc., 1952.

_____. *Sandwich Glass*. Wellesley Hills, Massachusetts: Lee Publications, 1939.

_____. *Victorian Glass*. Wellesley Hills, Massachusetts: Lee Publications, 1944.

Lee, Ruth Webb and James H. Rose. *American Glass Cup Plates*. Wellesley Hills, Massachusetts: Lee Publications, 1948.

Lindsey, Bessie M. *American Historical Glass*. Rutland, Vermont: Charles E. Tuttle Co., 1967.

Lovell, Russell A., Jr. *The Cape Cod Story of Thornton W. Burgess*. Taunton, Massachusetts: Thornton W. Burgess Society, Inc., and William S. Sullwold Publishing, 1974.

_____. *Sandwich; A Cape Cod Town*. Sandwich, Massachusetts: Town of Sandwich Massachusetts Archives and Historical Center, 1984.

Mackay, James. *Glass Paperweights*. New York, New York: The Viking Press, Inc., 1973.

Manheim, Frank J. *A Garland of Weights*. New York, New York: Farrar, Straus and Giroux, 1967.

Manley, C. C. *British Glass*. Des Moines, Iowa: Wallace-Homestead Book Co., 1968.

Manley, Cyril. *Decorative Victorian Glass*. New York, New York: Van Nostrand Reinhold Company, 1981.

Mannoni, Edith. *Opalines*. Paris, France: Éditions Ch. Massin, n.d.

McKearin, George S. and Helen McKearin. *American Glass*. New York, New York: Crown Publishers, Inc., 1941.

McKearin, Helen and George S. McKearin. *Two Hundred Years of American Blown Glass*. New York, New York: Bonanza Books, 1949.

McKearin, Helen and Kenneth M. Wilson. *American Bottles & Flasks and Their Ancestry*. New York, New York: Crown Publishers, Inc., 1978.

Measell, James. *Greentown Glass; The Indiana Tumbler and Goblet Company*. Grand Rapids, Michigan: The Grand Rapids Public Museum with the Grand Rapids Museum Association, 1979.

Metz, Alice Hulett. *Early American Pattern Glass*. Columbus, Ohio: Spencer-Walker Press, 1965.

_____. *Much More Early American Pattern Glass*. Columbus, Ohio: Spencer-Walker Press, 1970.

Millard, S. T. *Goblets II*. Holton, Kansas: Gossip Printers and Publishers, 1940.

Miller, Robert W. *Mary Gregory and Her Glass*. Des Moines, Iowa: Wallace-Homestead Book Co., 1972.

Moore, N. Hudson. *Old Glass*. New York, New York: Tudor Publishing Co., 1924.

Mulch, Dwight. "John D. Larkin and Company: From Factory to Family," *The Antique Trader Weekly*, June 24, 1984, pp. 92–94.

Neal, L. W. and D. B. Neal. *Pressed Glass Salt Dishes of the Lacy Period 1825-1850*. Philadelphia, Pennsylvania: L. W. and D. B. Neal, 1962.

Pearson, J. Michael and Dorothy T. Pearson. *American Cut Glass Collections*. Miami, Florida: The Franklin Press, Inc., 1969.

Pearson, J. Michael and Dorothy T. Pearson. *American Cut Glass for the Discriminating Collector*. Miami, Florida: The Franklin Press, Inc., 1965.

Pepper, Adeline. *The Glass Gaffers of New Jersey*. New York, New York: Charles Scribner's Sons, 1971.

Peterson, Arthur G. *Glass Patents and Patterns*. Sanford, Florida: Celery City Printing Co., 1973.

_____. *Glass Salt Shakers: 1,000 Patterns*. Des Moines, Iowa: Wallace-Homestead Book Co., 1960.

Raycraft, Don and Carol Raycraft. *Early American Lighting*. Des Moines, Iowa: Wallace-Homestead Book Co., n.d.

Revi, Albert Christian. *American Art Nouveau Glass*. Exton, Pennsylvania: Schiffer Publishing, Ltd., 1981.

_____. *American Cut and Engraved Glass*. Nashville, Tennessee: Thomas Nelson Inc., 1972.

_____. *American Pressed Glass and Figure Bottles*. Nashville, Tennessee: Thomas Nelson Inc., 1972.

_____. *Nineteenth Century Glass*. Exton, Pennsylvania: Schiffer Publishing, Ltd., 1967.

Righter, Miriam. *Iowa City Glass*. Des Moines, Iowa: Wallace-Homestead Book Co., 1966.

Robertson, Frank E. "New Evidence from Sandwich Glass Fragments," *The Magazine Antiques*, October 1982, pp. 818–823.

Robertson, R. A. *Chats on Old Glass*. New York, New York: Dover Publications, Inc., 1969. Revised and enlarged by Kenneth M. Wilson.

Rose, James H. *The Story of American Pressed Glass of the Lacy Period 1825-1850*. Corning, New York: The Corning Museum of Glass, 1954.

Rushlight Club. *Early Lighting; A Pictorial Guide*. Talcottville, Connecticut: 1972.

Sandwich Glass Museum. *The Sandwich Glass Museum Collection*. Sandwich, Massachusetts: Sandwich Glass Museum, 1969.

Sauzay, A. *Wonders of Art and Archaeology; Wonders of Glass Making*. New York, New York: Charles Scribner's Sons, 1885.

Schwartz, Marvin D. *American Glass from the Pages of Antiques; Blown and Moulded*. (Vol. I) Princeton, New Jersey: The Pyne Press, 1974.

Smith, Allan B. and Helen B. Smith. *One Thousand Individual Open Salts Illustrated*. Litchfield, Maine: The Country House, 1972.

Smith, Allan B. and Helen B. Smith. *650 More Individual Open Salts Illustrated*. Litchfield, Maine: The Country House, 1973.

Smith, Allan B. and Helen B. Smith. *The Third Book of Individual Open Salts Illustrated*. Litchfield, Maine: The Country House, 1976.

Smith, Allan B. and Helen B. Smith. *Individual Open Salts Illustrated*. Litchfield, Maine: The Country House, n.d.

Smith, Allan B. and Helen B. Smith. *Individual Open Salts Illustrated; 1977 Annual*. Litchfield, Maine: The Country House, 1977.

Smith, Frank R. and Ruth E. Smith. *Miniature Lamps*. New York, New York: Thomas Nelson Inc., 1968.

Spillman, Jane Shadel. *American and European Pressed Glass in The Corning Museum of Glass*. Corning, New York: The Corning Museum of Glass, 1981.

_____. *Glass Bottles, Lamps & Other Objects*. New York, New York: Alfred A. Knopf, Inc., 1983.

_____. *Glass Tableware, Bowls & Vases*. New York, New York: Alfred A. Knopf, Inc., 1982.

_____. "Pressed-Glass Designs in the United States and Europe," *The Magazine Antiques*, July 1983, pp. 130–139.

Stanley, Mary Louise. *A Century of Glass Toys*. Manchester, Vermont: Forward's Color Productions, Inc., n.d.

Stetson, Nelson M. *Booklet No. 6; Stetson Kindred of America*. Campbello, Massachusetts: 1923.

Stow, Charles Messer. *The Deming Jarves Book of Designs*. Yarmouth, Massachusetts: The Register Press, 1925.

Swan, Frank H. *Portland Glass*. Des Moines, Iowa: Wallace-Homestead Book Company, 1949. Revised and enlarged by Marion Dana.

_____. *Portland Glass Company*. Providence, Rhode Island: The Roger Williams Press, 1939.

Taylor, Katrina V. H. "Russian Glass in the Hillwood Museum." *The Magazine Antiques*, July 1983, pp. 140–145.

Teleki, Gloria Roth. *The Baskets of Rural America*. New York, New York: E. P. Dutton & Co., Inc., 1975.

The Toledo Museum of Art. *Art in Glass*. Toledo, Ohio: The Toledo Museum of Art, 1969.

_____. *The New England Glass Company 1818-1888*. Toledo, Ohio: The Toledo Museum of Art, 1963.

Thuro, Catherine M. V. *Oil Lamps; The Kerosene Era in North America*. Des Moines, Iowa: Wallace-Homestead Book Co., 1976.

_____. *Oil Lamps II; Glass Kerosene Lamps*. Paducah, Kentucky and Des Moines, Iowa: Collector Books and Wallace-Homestead Book Co., 1983.

Thwing, Leroy. *Flickering Flames*. Rutland, Vermont: Charles E. Tuttle Company, 1974.

Towne, Sumner. "Mike Grady's Last Pot," *Yankee*, March 1968, pp. 84, 85, 136–139.

VanRensselaer, Stephen. *Early American Bottles & Flasks*.

Stratford, Connecticut: J. Edmund Edwards, 1971.

Vuilleumier, Marion. *Cape Cod; a Pictorial History*. Norfolk, Virginia, 1982.

Walsh, Lavinia. "The Romance of Sandwich Glass," *The Cape Cod Magazine*, July 1926, pp. 9, 26.

_____. "Old Boston and Sandwich Glassworks . . . .," *Ceramic Age*, December 1950, pp. 16, 17, 34.

Watkins, Lura Woodside. *American Glass and Glassmaking*. New York, New York: Chanticleer Press, 1950.

_____. *Cambridge Glass 1818 to 1888*. New York, New York: Bramhall House, 1930.

Webber, Norman W. *Collecting Glass*. New York, New York: Arco Publishing Company, Inc., 1973.

Webster, Noah. *An American Dictionary of the English Language*. Springfield, Massachusetts: George and Charles Merriam, 1847. Revised.

_____. *An American Dictionary of the English Language*. Springfield, Massachusetts: George and Charles Merriam, 1859. Revised and enlarged by Chauncey A. Goodrich.

_____. *An American Dictionary of the English Language*. Springfield, Massachusetts: G. & C. Merriam, 1872. Revised and enlarged by Chauncey A. Goodrich and Noah Porter.

Wetz, Jon and Jacqueline Wetz. *The Co-operative Glass Company Sandwich, Massachusetts: 1888*-1891. Sandwich, Massachusetts: Barn Lantern Publishing, 1976.

Williams, Lenore Wheeler. *Sandwich Glass*. Bridgeport, Connecticut: The Park City Eng. Co., 1922.

Wilson, Kenneth M. *New England Glass & Glassmaking*. New York, New York: Thomas Y. Crowell Company, 1972.

CATALOGS

A. L. Blackmer Co. Rich Cut Glass 1906–1907. Shreveport, Louisiana: The American Cut Glass Association, reprinted in 1982.

Amberina; 1884 New England Glass Works; 1917 Libbey Glass Company. Toledo, Ohio: Antique & Historical Glass Foundation, reprinted in 1970.

Averbeck Rich Cut Glass Catalog No. 104, The. Berkeley, California: Cembura & Avery Publishers, reprinted in 1973.

Boston & Sandwich Glass Co., Boston. Wellesley Hills, Massachusetts: Lee Publications, reprinted in 1968.

Boston & Sandwich Glass Co. Price List. Collection of the Sandwich Glass Museum, Sandwich Historical Society, Sandwich, Massachusetts, n.d.

Catalog of 700 Packages Flint Glass Ware Manufactured by the Cape Cod Glass Works, to be Sold at the New England Trade Sale, Wednesday, July 14, 1859 at 9½ O'clock. Collection of The Corning Museum of Glass Library, Corning, New York, 1859.

C. Dorflinger & Sons Cut Glass Catalog. Silver Spring, Maryland: Christian Dorflinger Glass Study Group, reprinted in 1981.

Collector's Paperweights; Price Guide and Catalog. Santa Cruz, California: Paperweight Press, 1983.

Cut Glass Produced by the Laurel Cut Glass Company. Shreveport, Louisiana: The American Cut Glass Associ-

ation, reprinted, n.d.

Eggington's Celebrated Cut Glass. Shreveport, Louisiana: The American Cut Glass Association, reprinted in 1982.

Empire Cut Glass Company, The. Shreveport, Louisiana: American Cut Glass Association, reprinted in 1980.

F. X. Parsche & Son Co. Shreveport, Louisiana: American Cut Glass Association, reprinted in 1981.

Glassware Catalogue No. 25 Gillinder & Sons, Inc. Spring City, Tennessee: Hillcrest Books, reprinted in 1974.

Higgins and Seiter Fine China and Cut Glass Catalog No. 13. New York, New York: Higgins and Seiter, n.d.

Illustrated Catalog of American Hardware of the Russell and Erwin Manufacturing Company 1865. Association for Preservation Technology, reprinted in 1980.

J. D. Bergen Co., The; Manufacturers of Rich Cut Glassware 1904–1905. Berkeley, California: Cembura & Avery Publishers, reprinted in 1973.

Lackawanna Cut Glass Co. Shreveport, Louisiana: The American Cut Glass Association, reprinted, n.d.

Launay Hautin & Cie. Collection de dessins representant . . . Collection of The Corning Museum of Glass Library, Corning, New York, n.d.

Launay Hautin & Cie. Des Fabriques de Baccarat, St. Louis, Choisey et Bercy. Collection of The Corning Museum of Glass Library, Corning, New York, n.d.

Launay Hautin & Cie. Repertoire des Articles compris dans la Collection . . . Collection of The Corning Museum of Glass Library, Corning, New York, 1844.

Launay Hautin & Cie. Usages principaux pour services de table . . . Collection of The Corning Museum of Glass Library, Corning, New York, n.d.

Libbey Glass Co., The; Cut Glass June 1st, 1896. Toledo, Ohio: Antique & Historical Glass Foundation, reprinted in 1968.

List of Glass Ware Manufactured by Cape Cod Glass Company. Collection of the Sandwich Glass Museum, Sandwich Historical Society, Sandwich, Massachusetts, n.d.

M'Kee Victorial Glass; Five Complete Glass Catalogs from 1859/60 to 1871. New York, New York: Dover Publications, Inc., reprinted in 1981.

Monroe Cut Glass. Shreveport, Louisiana: American Cut Glass Association, reprinted, n.d.

Morey, Churchill & Morey Pocket Guide to 1880 Table Settings. Watkins Glen, New York: Century House, reprinted, n.d.

Mt. Washington Glass Co. Clinton, Maryland: Leonard E. Padgett, reprinted in 1976.

Mt. Washington Glass Company (cut glassware). Collection of The Corning Museum of Glass Library, Corning, New York, n.d.

Mt. Washington Glass Company; Crystal Gas Fixtures. Collection of The Corning Museum of Glass Library, Corning, New York, n.d.

Mt. Washington Glass Works (glass prisms and beads). Collection of The Corning Museum of Glass Library, Corning, New York, n.d.

Mt. Washington Glass Works Price List. Collection of The Corning Museum of Glass Library, Corning, New York, n.d.

New England Glass Company. Collection of The Corning Museum of Glass Library, Corning, New York, n.d.

New England Glass Company (list of glassware). Collection of The Corning Museum of Glass Library, Corning, New York, n.d.

Picture Book of Authentic Mid-Victorian Gas Lighting Fixtures; A Reprint of the Historic Mitchell, Vance & Co. Catalog, ca. 1876, with Over 1000 Illustrations. Mineola, New York: Dover Publications, Inc., reprinted in 1984.

Public Auction Richard A. Bourne Company, Inc. Boston, Massachusetts: The Nimrod Press, Inc., 1970-1985.

Quaker City Cut Glass Co. Shreveport, Louisiana: American Cut Glass Association, n.d.

Rich Cut Glass Pitkin & Brooks. Berkeley, California: Cembura & Avery Publishers, reprinted in 1973.

Sandwich Glass Patterns. West Englewood, New Jersey: Bernadine Forgett, n.d.

Taylor Bros. & Company, Inc., Manufacturers of Cut Glass. Shreveport, Louisiana: American Cut Glass Association, n.d.

BUSINESS DIRECTORIES

Boston City Directories. 1789-1891.

Resident and Business Directory of Bourne, Falmouth and Sandwich, Massachusetts. Hopkinton, Massachusetts: A. E. Foss & Co., 1900

NEWSPAPERS AND TRADE PAPERS

*Academy Breezes. 1884-*1886.

Acorn, The. Sandwich, Massachusetts: The Sandwich Historical Society, 1967-1985.

American Collector. New York, New York: Educational Publishing Corporation, 1933-1946.

Barnstable Patriot. 1830-1869.

Barnstable Patriot, The. 1869-1905, 1912-1916, 1918-1923.

Bourne Pioneer, The. 1906-1907.

Brockton Searchlight, The. 1909.

Cape Cod Advocate, and Nautical Intelligencer. 1851-1864.

Cape Cod Gazette. 1870-1872.

Casino Bulletin. 1884-1885.

Chronicle of the Early American Industries Association, The. Flushing, New York: Leon S. Case, January 1938.

Crockery & Glass Journal. New York, New York: George Whittemore & Company, 1885-1890.

Crockery Journal. New York, New York: George Whittemore & Company, 1874-1884.

Glass Club Bulletin, The. The National Early American Glass Club, 1938-1985.

Hyannis Patriot, The. 1908-1909, 1916-1918, 1923-1925.

Independent, The. 1895-1908.

Sandwich Collector, The. East Sandwich, Massachusetts: McCue Publications, 1984-1985.

Sandwich Independent. 1920-1921.

Sandwich Independent, The. 1908-1909.

Sandwich Mechanic and Family Visitor. 1851.

Sandwich Observer. 1846-1851.

Sandwich Observer, The. 1884-1895, 1910-1911.

Sandwich Review, The. 1889-1890.

Seaside Press, The. 1873-1880.

Village Broadsider, The. 1978-1985.

Weekly Review, The. 1881-1882.

Yarmouth Register and Barnstable County Advertiser. 1836-1839.

Yarmouth Register and Barnstable County Weekly Advertiser. 1839-1846.

Yarmouth Register. 1849-1906.

BARLOW-KAISER
SANDWICH GLASS
PRICE GUIDE
for pieces in perfect condition

SECOND EDITION

to be used with Volumes 3 and 4 of
THE GLASS INDUSTRY IN SANDWICH
and
A GUIDE TO SANDWICH GLASS

INTRODUCTION TO PRICE GUIDE

It is most important to determine the condition of a glass item before you purchase it. We are often so fascinated by a good "find" that we miss its obvious condition. The prices in this guide are for items that are in perfect, or *mint*, condition. *Mint condition* is an article of glass that is pristine. It has no defects. If there is roughage only in places where there are mold marks, it is still considered to be mint, because if the item was good enough to pass inspection at the time of production, it is good enough to be called mint today. Shear marks (often called "straw marks"), caused by cutting through a glob of glass while it was hot, do not detract from value. They are a fact of construction procedure. Manufacturing errors, such as annealing marks, bent or twisted pieces, off-center pieces, underfilled or overfilled molds, and overheating, add character to a piece of glass. However, the mint condition status of the glass is not affected. Rapid reductions in pricing are caused by damage after the time of manufacture in the following order, using the 100% value of a mint item as a base.

CONDITION	MAXIMUM VALUE OF MINT
CHIPPED Damage serious enough to penetrate into the body of an article, but small or shallow enough so that it cannot be glued back or replaced.	80%
BRUISED When an article has been struck with enough force to send cracks in several directions, penetrating the surface at the center.	60%
CRACKED When the glass is split through one or more layers, caused by a blow, a change in temperature, or stress in the glass at the time of manufacture. This is the first stage of deterioration, leading to eventual destruction. Value is seriously affected	50%
BROKEN An article is broken when it is in two pieces, even though one of the pieces may only be the tip of a scallop, or the corner of a base, or the peg of a lamp font. If one piece must be glued back in order to make the article whole, the article is broken and its value must be reduced accordingly.	25%

An unusually rare article, even though broken, must be considered for purchase regardless of price, if the serious collector is to have an example of that article.

VASES AND FLOWER CONTAINERS

A single vase is worth less than 50% of a matching pair. When you are pricing vases, make sure you have a matching pair and not two single vases. Unlike candlesticks and lamps, vases that were pressed were made in single colors only.

Photo No.	Clear	Clambroth (Alabaster)	Opaque White	Canary	Amber	Blue	Amethyst	Green	Unusual Color
3001 a	45 ea.			160 ea.		180 ea.	180 ea.		
b				12 ea.		12 ea.	12 ea.	15 ea.	12 ea. ruby
3002				400 pr.			550 pr.		
3003		200 ea. fiery opalescent			200 ea.	160 ea.	160 ea.		250 ea. lime green
3004		200 ea. fiery opalescent			200 ea.	160 ea.	160 ea.		250 ea. lime green
3005	15 ea.			60 ea.		60 ea.	75 ea.		
3006	20 ea.								
3007	115 ea.								
3008	1200 pr.								
3009	85 ea.								
3010	95 ea.								
3011	95 ea.								
3012	115 ea.								
3013	100 ea.								
3014	60 ea.	110 ea.	110 ea.	150 ea.		150 ea.	175 ea.	175 ea.	200 ea.
3015	135 pr.	300 pr.	300 pr.	450 pr.		450 pr.	500 pr.	500 pr.	600 pr.
3016	18 ea.					75 ea.	75 ea.	85 ea.	
3017	400 pr.			1200 pr.		1500 pr.	1800 pr.	2000 pr.	
3018	200 ea.			500 ea.		875 ea.	900 ea.	1000 ea.	
3019	600 pr.					2200 pr.		2400 pr.	
3020							2400 pr.		
3021	65 ea.			450 ea.	1000 ea.	875 ea.	650 ea.	1000 ea.	1200+ ea.
3022	65 ea.			450 ea.	1000 ea.	875 ea.	650 ea.	1000 ea.	1200+ ea.
3023	65 ea.			450 ea.	1000 ea.	875 ea.	650 ea.	1000 ea.	1200+ ea.
3024	85 ea.								
3025				875 ea.		1000 ea.			
3026				950 pr.	1000 pr.	1000 pr.	1000 pr.	1200 pr.	
3027		750 ea.		900 ea.			1000 ea.		
3028						875 ea.	1000 ea.		
3029				550 ea.		850 ea.		950 ea.	
3030						2400 pr.			
3031				550 ea.					
3032				875 ea.		1000 ea.			
3033	240 pr.	800 pr.		950 pr.		1400 pr.	1400 pr.	1800 pr.	
3034				1000 pr.		1450 pr.	1450 pr.	1850 pr.	
3035				450 ea.			750 ea.		
3036				450 ea.			750 ea.		
3037 a				550 ea.			750 ea.		
b							875 ea.		
3038		350 ea.		550 ea.					
3039				1800 pr.		2500 pr.		2600 pr.	
3040				850 ea.		1100 ea.		1200 ea.	
3041		700 ea. fiery opalescent	700 ea.	750 ea.				950 ea.	

Photo No.	Clear	Clambroth (Alabaster)	Opaque White	Canary	Amber	Blue	Amethyst	Green	Unusual Color
3042 a	90 ea.			400 ea.		750 ea.	750 ea.	825 ea.	
b	100 ea.			425 ea.		775 ea.	775 ea.	850 ea.	
3043 a						450 pr.			
b						225 ea.		350 ea.	
3044 a						450 pr.			
b		225 ea. with fitting	300 ea. with fitting			250 ea. with fitting	350 ea. with fitting	350 ea. with fitting	
3045		75 ea.							
3046 a						225 ea. blue and white		225 ea. green and white	
b						275 ea. blue and white		275 ea. green and white	
3047						225 ea. blue and white		225 ea. green and white	
3048 a		160 ea.				185 ea.	225 ea.		
b				200 ea.		225 ea.			

Photo No.		
3049	600 ea.	pink to white to clear Overlay, gilded
3050	150 ea.	clear
	300 ea.	opal, decorated
3051	225 ea.	
3052	200 ea.	
3053	200 ea.	
3054	600 the set	
3055	40 ea.	
3056	40 ea.	
3057	40 ea.	
3058	60 ea.	
3059	100 ea.	
3060	125 pr.	
3061	50 ea.	
3062	60 ea.	
3063	60 ea.	
3064	60 ea.	
3065	40 ea.	
3066	—	
3067	—	
3068	—	
3069	22 ea.	
3070	28 ea.	
3071	50 ea.	
3072	50 ea.	
3073	85 ea.	
3074	85 ea.	
3075	95 ea.	
3076	140 ea.	undecorated
3077	250 ea.	decorated, blue ground
	250 ea.	decorated, brown ground
	300 ea.	decorated, lilac ground
	450 ea.	decorated, colored flowers, white ground

Photo No.		
3078 a	65 ea.	
b	55 ea.	
c	45 ea.	
3079	125 ea.	
3080	95 ea.	
3081	—	
3082	225 ea.	
3083	400 ea.	
3084	600 ea.	
3085	—	
3086	—	
3087	600 ea.	
3088 a	250	stand only
b	600 ea.	
c	600 ea.	
3089 a	40 ea.	
b	28 ea.	
c	20 ea.	
3090	85 ea.	
3091	100 ea.	
3092	30 ea.	
3093	35 ea.	
3094	30 ea.	
3095	35 ea.	
3096	50 ea.	
3097	15 ea.	
3098	65 ea.	
3099	85 ea.	fiery opalescent
3100	115 ea.	fiery opalescent

COLOGNES

Cologne bottles used on dressing tables have glass stoppers. Half the value of a cologne is in its stopper.

Photo No.	Clear	Clambroth (Alabaster)	Opaque White	Canary	Amber	Blue	Amethyst	Green
3101	110 ea.	350 ea.		350 ea.		1400 ea.		2800 ea.
3102	110 ea.	350 ea.		350 ea.		1400 ea.		2800 ea.
3103	110 ea.			350 ea.				
3104				400 ea.		950 ea.		
3105	90 ea.			275 ea.				
3106	115 ea.		400 ea.	500 ea.				
3107					450 ea.	450 ea.		500 ea.
3108	190 pr.	450 pr. fiery opalescent			450 pr.			600 pr.
3109	75 ea.	175 ea. fiery opalescent			175 ea.			250 ea.
3110				250 ea.	250 ea.	275 ea.		300 ea.
3111	80 ea.					160 ea.		
3112				175 ea.	175 ea.	225 ea.	250 ea.	
3113				275 ea.		400 ea.		500 ea.
3114						500 ea.		
3115					500 ea.			

Photo No.	Clear	Clambroth (Alabaster)	Opaque White	Canary	Amber	Blue	Amethyst	Green
3116			300 ea.					
3117				200 ea.		225 ea.		
3118 a						250 ea.	275 ea.	350 ea.
b	50 ea.			200 ea.				
3119						250 ea.		350 ea.
3120				225 ea.				350 ea.
3121 a						450 ea.		
b		45 ea.				65 ea.		
c		225 ea. with fitting	300 ea. with fitting			250 ea. with fitting	350 ea. with fitting	350 ea. with fitting
3122								160 ea. green and white
3123						185 ea. blue and white		185 ea. green and white
3124								350 ea.
3125		225 ea.				300 ea.		350 ea.
3126								850 ea.

Photo No.		
3127	450 ea.	
3128	—	
3129	150 ea.	
3130	160 ea.	with stopper
3131	115 ea.	
3132	135 ea.	
3133	150 ea.	
3134	110 ea.	
3135	250 ea.	blue to clear Overlay
3136	250 ea.	blue to clear Overlay
	300 ea.	ruby to clear Overlay
3137	325 ea.	blue to clear Overlay
3138	250 ea.	blue to clear Overlay
3139	300 ea.	blue to clear Overlay
	350 ea.	ruby to clear Overlay
3140	400 ea.	blue to clear Overlay
	400 ea.	ruby to clear Overlay
	600 ea.	green to clear Overlay
3141	400 ea.	blue to clear Overlay
3142	400 ea.	blue to clear Overlay
	450 ea.	ruby to clear Overlay
3143	875 ea.	ruby to clear Overlay
3144	—	
3145	575 ea.	ruby to clear Overlay
3146	650 ea.	amethyst to clear Overlay
3147	575 ea.	ruby to clear Overlay
3148	600 ea.	ruby to clear Overlay
3149	450 ea.	ruby to clear Overlay, with correct stopper
3150	500 ea.	ruby to clear Overlay
3151 a	60 ea.	ruby to clear Overlay
b	60 ea.	blue to clear Overlay

Photo No.		
3152	600 pr.	blue to clear Overlay
	750 pr.	ruby to clear Overlay
	875 pr.	green to clear Overlay
3153	110 ea.	clear
3154	300 ea.	blue to clear Overlay
	350 ea.	ruby to clear Overlay
	400 ea.	green to clear Overlay
3155	250 ea.	ruby to clear Overlay
3156	500 ea.	ruby to clear Overlay
3157	875 ea.	ruby to clear Overlay
3158	225 ea.	pink to white to clear Overlay
3159	475 ea.	pink to white to clear Overlay
3160	95 ea.	ruby stained
3161	95 ea.	ruby stained
3162	95 ea.	ruby stained
3163	95 ea.	ruby stained
3164	65 ea.	ruby stained, with correct stopper
3165	200 pr.	ruby stained
3166	225 ea.	ruby stained
3167	175 ea.	clear Overshot
	275 ea.	blue Overshot
	275 ea.	pink Overshot
3168	275 ea.	blue Overshot
	275 ea.	pink Overshot
3169	85 ea.	
3170	65 ea.	
3171	325 ea.	green threads on green
3172	185 ea.	ruby threads on clear, engraved
3173	185 ea.	ruby threads on clear, with correct stopper

STOPPERS

A container that has its correct stopper often will double in value. The purchase of stoppers known to be Sandwich is an investment that will pay handsomely from time to time.

Photo No.	Clear	Clambroth (Alabaster)	Opaque White	Canary	Amber	Blue	Ruby	Amethyst	Green
3174	2–3 ea.								
3175	2–3 ea.								
3176 a	2–3 ea.				7 ea.				
b					5 ea.				
c					5 ea.				
3177	15 ea.				40 ea.	28 ea.		30 ea.	
3178	15 ea.					28 ea.		30 ea.	
3179	20 ea.								
3180 a	—								
b	15 ea.								
3181	15 ea.					50 ea.			
3182	15 ea.								
3183 a	7 ea.								
b	7 ea.								
c	5 ea.								
d	5 ea.								
3184	18 ea.								
3185	5 ea.								

Photo No.	Clear	Clambroth (Alabaster)	Opaque White	Canary	Amber	Blue	Ruby	Amethyst	Green
3186	4 ea.								
3187	4 ea.								
3188	4 ea.								
3189									875 pale green
3190 a	3 ea.								5 ea. pale green
b	4 ea.								7 ea. pale green
c	3 ea.								5 ea. pale green
3191					1000				
3192					5 ea.				
3193				10 ea.	5 ea.		20 ea.	25 ea.	
3194	3 ea.								
3195 a	—								
b	40 ea.								
c	35 ea.								
d	35 ea.								
e	35 ea.								
3196	18 ea.								
3197	20 ea.								
3198	30 ea.								
3199	40 ea.								
3200	20 ea.								
3201	6 ea.								
3202	4 ea.								
3203 a	—								
b	4 ea.								
c	4 ea.			10 ea.	15 ea.	15 ea.		15 ea.	
3204 a	8 ea.			20 ea.	20 ea.	25 ea.	50 ea.	25 ea.	60 ea. dark green
b	8 ea.								
3205	10 ea.								
3206 a	8 ea.			15 ea.					
b	8 ea.			15 ea.					
c	8 ea.		20 ea.		20 ea.				
3207	5 ea.			15 ea.	15 ea.	18 ea.			
3208 a	5 ea.			15 ea.	15 ea.	18 ea.			
b	8 ea.			15 ea.					
3209 a	8 ea.								
b	8 ea.			18 ea.		18 ea.			25 ea.
c	8 ea.			18 ea.		18 ea.		25 ea.	
d	8 ea.			20 ea.	20 ea.	25 ea.	50 ea.	25 ea.	60 ea.
3210 a	15 ea.			25 ea.					
b	15 ea.				35 ea.				45 ea.
c	15 ea.				35 ea.				45 ea.
3211		25 ea.				45 ea.			60 ea. custard
3212 a									50 ea.
b						35 ea.			
c						35 ea.			
3213	5 ea.			12 ea.	12 ea.	15 ea.		18 ea.	
3214	5 ea.				12 ea.				

Photo No.	Clear	Clambroth (Alabaster)	Opaque White	Canary	Amber	Blue	Ruby	Amethyst	Green
3215	5 ea.			12 ea.	12 ea.	15 ea.		18 ea.	
3216	8 ea.			18 ea.		18 ea.		25 ea.	25 ea.
3217	5 ea.			12 ea.	12 ea.	15 ea.		18 ea.	
3218 a	10 ea.								
b	12 ea.								
c	15 ea.								
d	15 ea.								

Photo No.		
3219 a	15 ea.	
b	18 ea.	
c	22 ea.	ruby threads on clear
d	12 ea.	
3220 a	15 ea.	
b	20 ea.	
c	15 ea.	
3221 a	20 ea.	ruby threads on clear
b	25 ea.	ruby threads on clear
c	20 ea.	ruby threads on clear
d	20 ea.	ruby threads on clear
3222 a	100 ea.	
b	110 ea.	
3223 a	90 ea.	
b	100 ea.	
3224	—	

BALLS

Photo No.		
3225	150	
3226	140	
3227	150 ea.	
3228	150	
3229	175	
3230	60	
3231	60	
3232	50	
3233 a	90	
b	—	
3234	500	with extension
3235	500	with extension
3236	160	
3237	15 ea.	
3238	12 ea.	
3239 a	12 ea.	
b	180	
3240	12 ea.	
3241	—	
3242	45 ea.	

COVERED CONTAINERS

Little value remains to a container that has lost its cover. Keeping covers in pristine condition guarantees maximum return on the dollar spent for containers.

Photo No.	Clear	Clambroth (Alabaster)	Fiery Opalescent	Opaque White	Canary	Amber	Blue	Amethyst	Green
3243	3500				6500		7500		
3244	350				500		600		
3245	4000				7500		8500		
3246	—								
3247	4000				7500		8500		
3248	—								
3249	350				500		600		
3250	3500				6500				
3251							9000		
3252	—								
3253	600	750		800	1200		1800		2800
3254	—								
3255				350			550		
3256				250					
3257				300					
3258				400 with cover					
3259					1200		1100	1200	
3260		1000		1500			2500		3500
3261 a		1000		1200			2000	500	
b		800		1000			1500	400	
c		600		800			1100	300	
3262		600		800			1100	300	
3263 a		1000					1800	950	
b	—								
3264		90							
3265	250						1600		2200
3266	300						1400		1800
3267 a	—								
b	300						1400		1800
3268 a	200	500					1200		1500
b	50	275					375		500
3269	250	350			900		900		1500
3270	300	375		450	1200		900		1500
3271 a	45	110		125	550		375		500
b	50								
3272	190 with cover						1000 with cover		
3273	90				875		1000		
3274	110			275					
3275	50								
3276	85 ea.			200 ea.	375 ea.				
3277 a	—								
b				50					
3278	425						1000	1000	
3279				300			575	650	
3280 a	110				300		575		575
b	110				275		525		525

Photo No.	Clear	Clambroth (Alabaster)	Fiery Opalescent	Opaque White	Canary	Amber	Blue	Amethyst	Green
3281	—								
3282 a	22	45			85		115		160
b	22	50			90		135		175
3283				150				180	
3284	85	180	200		225	250	325	375	
3285					325				450
3286	—								
3287							750		
3288	—								
3289	80	225			375		575		
3290	425 ruby to clear Overlay								
3291	65		110					225	
3292 a	40		125						
b	40		125						
3293 a	40		125				225		
b	40		125						
3294 a	40		125						
b	40		125				225		
3295			35						
3296				28 ea.					
3297				135					
3298				60					
3299	50 ea.	80 ea.		80 ea.	90 ea.		110 ea.	135 ea.	150 ea.
3300	—								

TOYS

Glass toys made during the Nineteenth Century were intended for children's play. Expect to find more roughage than is found on adult tableware. The value does not drop as rapidly when toys are chipped or damaged.

Photo No.	Clear	Clambroth (Alabaster)	Fiery Opalescent	Opaque White	Canary	Amber	Blue	Amethyst	Green
3301	400 with burner						875 with burner		
3302	450 with burner						1000 with burner		
3302 a	25						60		
b	475 with burner						1500 with burner		
3304	450 with burner								
3305	500 with burner						1200 with burner		
3306	1000 complete								
3307	70								
3308 a	100								
b	185								
3309	100								

Photo No.	Clear	Clambroth (Alabaster)	Opaque White	Canary	Amber	Blue	Ruby	Amethyst	Green
3310	250								
3311	450						600		
3312	250						500		
3313	250						500		
3314	250						500		
3315	425				1200				
3316	350 the set						1100 the set	1200 the set	
3317	250 the set		900 the set		700 the set		1000 the set	1100 the set	
3318	160 ea.		375 ea.		400 ea.		500 ea.	550 ea.	
3319	225 the set				600 the set		900 the set	950 the set	
3320	38 ea.	65 ea.	90 ea.		125 ea.		150 ea.	165 ea.	200 ea.
3321 a	38 ea.	65 ea.	90 ea.		125 ea.		150 ea.	165 ea.	200 ea.
b	40 ea.	75 ea.	125 ea.		165 ea.		250 ea.	250 ea.	225 ea.
c	38 ea.	65 ea.	90 ea.		125 ea.		150 ea.	165 ea.	200 ea.
3322	425								
3323	18 ea.				90 ea.	150 ea.	110 ea.	110 ea.	150 ea.
3324	18 ea.				90 ea.	150 ea.	110 ea.	110 ea.	150 ea.
3325 a	18 ea.				100 ea.	160 ea.	120 ea.	120 ea.	175 ea.
b	28 ea.				125 ea.	175 ea.	150 ea.	150 ea.	200 ea.
3326	28				90	160	120	120	175
3327	28				90	160	120	120	175
3328 a	28 ea.						125 ea.	175 ea.	
b	35 ea. pressed handle						150 ea. pressed handle	150 ea. pressed handle	175 ea. pressed handle
	75 ea. applied handle						275 ea. applied handle	275 ea. applied handle	300 ea. applied handle
3329	35 ea.	80 ea.					150 ea.	175 ea.	150 ea.
3330	200								
3331	100								
3332	100								
3333	85								
3334	38 ea.	100 ea.					150 ea.	175 ea.	200 ea.
3335	38						150		200
3336 a	100 ea.		250 ea.				550 ea.	600 ea.	700 ea.
b	65 ea.		200 ea.				450 ea.	475 ea.	500 ea.
3337	150 the set				400 the set		550 the set	600 the set	
3338	75	150	275		300		400	450	
3339	75	150	275		300		400	450	
3340	75	150	225		300	600	400	600	
3341	75 ea.	150 ea.	225 ea.		300 ea.	600 ea.	400 ea.	600 ea.	
3342	60								
3343	60								
3344	75 ea.	150 ea.	275 ea.		500 ea.		550 ea.	600 ea.	700 ea.
3345	300 ea.				900 ea.		1000 ea.	1000 ea.	1000 ea.
3346 a	150 ea.								
b	225 ea.								
3347	300 with underplate		875 with underplate		875 with underplate		1200 with underplate	1300 with underplate	1400 with underplate
3348 a	110 ea.		200 ea.		200 ea.		225 ea.	250 ea.	300 ea.
b	90 ea.		175 ea.		175 ea.		200 ea.	225 ea.	275 ea.
3349	75 ea.		125 ea.		125 ea.		200 ea.		
3350	75 ea.		125 ea.		125 ea.		200 ea.		
3351	150				500		750	850	1000

Photo No.	Clear	Clambroth (Alabaster)	Fiery Opalescent	Opaque White	Canary	Amber	Blue	Amethyst	Green
3352	150								
3353 a	40 ea.								
b	75 ea.								
3354	150								
3355	150 the set								
3356	200 the set with box								
3357	150 the set								
3358 a	15 with cap								
b	20 with cover								
c	18 with stopper								
3359	18 ea.				50 ea.				
3360	200 pr.		750 pr.		650 pr.		900 pr.	1000 pr.	1400 pr.
3361	150 ea.		275 ea.		600 ea.		600 ea.	600 ea.	600 ea.

Photo No.

3362	50 ea.	multi-colored
3363	150	opaque white
3364	500	clear
3365	7500	clear
3366 a	250	canary
b	650	Vasa Murrhina
c	700	ruby
3367	150	Vasa Murrhina
3368	150	ruby to clear Overlay
3369	—	
3370 a	125	clear
b	125	clear
c	100	clear
d	125	clear
3371	250 ea.	ruby to clear Overlay

CREATIONS OF NICHOLAS LUTZ

Photo No.

3372	—
3373	—
3374	—
3375	—
3376	—
3377	—
3378	—
3379	—
3380	—

Photo No.	
3381	—
3382	—
3383	575
3384	900
3385	1000
3386	1000
3387	750
3388	1400
3389	—
3390	600
3391	600
3392	575
3393	1200 pr.
3394	600
3395	175
3396	700
3397	700
3398	300
3399	2000
3400	160
3401	90
3402	300 ea.
3403	7500
3404	95 ea.
3405	700
3406	50
3407	—
3408	90–150 ea.
3409	90–150 ea.
3410	90–150 ea.
3411	90–150 ea.
3412	—
3413	100
3414	100 ea. with documentation
3415	15
3416	—
3417	—

CANDLESTICKS

A single candlestick is worth less than 50% of a matching pair. In most instances, a two-color candlestick is more valuable than the same candlestick made in one color.

Photo No.	Clear	Clambroth (Alabaster)	Opaque White	Canary	Amber	Blue	Amethyst	Green	Unusual Color
4001	2500 ea.								
4002	—								
4003	450 pr.								
4004	450 pr.								
4005	175 ea.								
4006	150 ea.								
4007	450 pr.								
4008	600 ea.					1500 ea.			
4009	3500 ea.								
4010	325 pr. including inserts			750 pr. including inserts		1400 pr. including inserts			

Photo No.	Clear	Clambroth (Alabaster)	Opaque White	Canary	Amber	Blue	Amethyst	Green	Unusual Color
4011	375 pr.								
4012	375 pr.								
4013	700 pr.								
4014	500 pr.								
4015	200 pr.			600 pr.		700 pr.			
4016	80 ea.			200 ea.					600 + ea.
4017	200 pr.			450 pr.					
4018	100 ea.			250 ea.		325 ea.			
4019	225 pr.			400 pr.					
4020	85 ea.			140 ea.		300 ea.			
4021	175 pr.			375 pr.			700 pr.		
4022	85 ea.			140 ea.			325 ea.		
4023	250 pr.	450 pr.		600 pr.	800 pr.	800 pr. blue and white		1200 pr. green and white	1400 + pr.
4024	175 pr.			400 pr.	550 pr.	550 pr.	700 pr.	750 pr.	
4025 candlesticks	250 pr.								
4025 peg lamps	100 pr.								
4026	250 pr.			500 pr.		600 pr.	650 pr.		750 + pr.
4027	200 pr.	250 pr.		400 pr.	650 pr.	650 pr.	650 pr.	700 pr.	750 + pr.
4028	175 pr.			400 pr.	650 pr.	650 pr.	650 pr.	700 pr.	750 + pr.
4029	80 ea.			150 ea.		275 ea.	275 ea.		
4030	80 ea.			150 ea.		275 ea.	275 ea.		
4031	90 ea.			150 ea.					
4032	175 pr.	300 pr.	300 pr.	395 pr.	1000 pr.	550 pr.	600 pr.	750 pr.	800 + pr.
4033 a	95		500	950			1200		
b	125			1000			1500		
4034	—								
4035	—								
4036	90 ea.			140 ea.		250 ea.	250 ea.	300 ea.	400 + ea.
4037	90 ea.			140 ea.		250 ea.	250 ea.	300 ea.	400 + ea.
4038	125 ea.	175 ea.	200 ea.	325 ea.		400 ea. blue and white		800 ea. green and white	650 + ea.
4039 a	80 ea.					300 ea.		400 ea.	
b	125 ea.	175 ea.	200 ea.	325 ea.		450 ea.		600 ea.	500 + ea.
4040	125 ea.	175 ea.	200 ea.	325 ea.		450 ea.		600 ea.	500 + ea.
4041 a	175 ea.					500 ea. all blue / 450 ea. blue and white		650 ea. green and white	
b	150 ea.					350 ea. blue and white		500 ea. green and white	
c	175 ea.					500 ea. blue and white		700 ea. green and white	
4042	90 ea.			150 ea.	250 ea.	250 ea.	275 ea.	325 ea.	
4043	—								
4044 a	225		500		750	800	800	950	1000 +
b	20								
4045	400		800		1200	1200	1200	1400	1500 +
4046	125 pr.	225 pr.	250 pr.	600 pr.	800 pr.	900 pr.	1000 pr.	1000 pr.	1200 + pr.
4047	150 pr.	250 pr.	250 pr.	800 pr.	800 pr.	900 pr.	1000 pr.	1000 pr.	1200 + pr.
4048	200 pr.	300 pr.	400 pr.	800 pr.		1000 pr.	1200 pr.	1500 pr.	1600 + pr.
4049	800		2000	3500		4500	4500	5000	
4050		2000	2000	3000		4500	4500	5000	

Photo No.	Clear	Clambroth (Alabaster)	Opaque White	Canary	Amber	Blue	Amethyst	Green	Unusual Color
4051	125 ea.	175 ea.	200 ea.	225 ea.		300 ea.	300 ea.	400 ea.	
4052	200 pr.	400 pr.	450 pr.	800 pr.		800 pr.	800 pr.	900 pr.	
4053	90 ea.	150 ea.	200 ea.	225 ea.		300 ea.	300 ea.	400 ea.	
4054	350 pr.	650 pr.	700 pr.	900 pr.		1500 pr.	1500 pr.	2200 pr.	
4055	350 pr.	650 pr.	700 pr.	900 pr.		1500 pr.	1500 pr.	2200 pr.	
4056 a	125 ea.	275 ea.	300 ea.	400 ea.		600 ea.	600 ea.	800 ea.	
b						500 ea. blue and white		800 ea. green and white	
4057	—								
4058 a						550 ea. blue and white		875 ea. green and white	1200+ ea.
b	125 ea.	275 ea.	300 ea.	400 ea.		400 ea.	450 ea.	650 ea.	
4059						800 ea. blue and white, gilded			
4060	350 ea.					1200 ea. blue and white		2000 ea. green and white	
4061	300 ea.				700 ea.				
4062	—								
4063	140								
Fig. 5	500 ea. with socket								
4064	20								

INSULATORS

Photo No.		Photo No.	
4065	35–40 ea. with collar	Fig. 8	60
4066	90–110 ea. with cap and collar	4071	30
4067	16–20 ea. with collar	4072	—
4068	16–20 ea. with clamp	4073	250
4069	—	4074	—
4070	—	4075	—

OVERSHOT (FROSTED WARE)

Photo No.	Clear	Pink	Amber	Blue	Unusual Color
4076 a	200 ea.	700 ea.			
b	200 ea.	375 ea.			
4077	400 pr.	800 pr.		800 pr.	
4078	225 ea.	450 ea.			
4079 a	180 ea.	300 ea.			
b	160 ea.	280 ea.			
4080	75 ea.	250 ea.			
4081	75 ea.	280 ea.	450 ea.		
4082	90 ea.	250 ea.			

Photo No.	Clear	Pink	Amber	Blue	Unusual Color
4083	65–90 ea.	200–250 ea.			
4084 a	85 ea.	250 ea.		350 ea.	
b	135 ea.	300 ea.		350 ea.	
4085	125 ea.	250 ea.			
4086 a					240 ea. canary
b	110 ea.				
4087	75 ea.		135 ea.		
4088 a	75 ea.	135 ea.	150 ea.	175 ea.	
b	60 ea.	250 ea.		250 ea.	
c	60 ea.	200 ea.		200 ea.	
4089	95 ea.	135 ea.		175 ea.	350 ea. green
4090 a	160 ea.			300 ea.	
b	35 ea.			75 ea.	
4091 a	180 ea.			400 ea.	
b	160 ea.			300 ea.	
4092 a	100 ea.				400 ea. ruby
b	125 ea. amber handle			200 ea.	
4093	80 pr.	250 pr.			
4094 a	150 ea.				
b	140 ea.				
4095	150 the set	300 the set			
4096 a	45 ea.	135 ea.			
b	35 ea.	75 ea.			
c	75 ea.				
d	40 with stopper				
4097	25 ea.	65 ea.			
4098	90 ea.	160 ea.		200 ea.	
4099	65 ea.	110 ea.			
4100	135 ea.				250 ea. canary
4101	125 ea.				
4102	180 the set				
4103	75 ea.		160 ea.	175 ea.	
4104	35 the set	95 the set	110 the set	110 the set	
4105	35 the set	95 the set	110 the set	110 the set	
4106	110 ea.	225 ea.		250 ea.	
4107	300 the set				

VASA MURRHINA

Photo No.		Photo No.	
4108	300	4117	—
4109	—	4118	650
4110	90	4119	—
4111	—	4120	150
4112	450	4121	—
4113	100	4122	125
4114	110	4123	—
4115	—	4124	125
4116	160	4125	—

4126	—		4128	—
4127	—		4129	—

4130–4155 Cut or engraved by N. Packwood in Sandwich, but not *manufactured* by Packwood.

4156–4176 Cut or engraved by J. B. Vodon and Son in Sandwich, but not *manufactured* by Vodon.

LATE BLOWN WARE

There are five levels of value.

- The price based on the type of article and its etched or engraved design.
- The addition of a monogram that cannot be traced back to the original owner of the article reduces the base price.
- The addition of a monogram with documentation that traces the object back to the original owner adds to the base price.
- A presentation piece that is completely documented, with a monogram, complete name, date, or special design, is valued significantly higher than any of the above.
- Colored pieces are very scarce and should be priced accordingly.

Photo No.		Photo No.		Photo No.	
4177	45	4206	150	4232	38
4178	20	4207	110	4233 a	125
4179	20	4208	185	b	25
4180 a	20	4209	20	4234	125
b	18	4210	22	4235	12 ea.
c	15	4211	15 ea. clear	4236	55
4181	20		85 ea. amber	4237	75 the set
4182	20	4212 a	10	4238	65
4183	25	b	12	4239	150
4184	55	c	12	4240	65
4185	165 for jar	4213 a	65	4241	50
4186	25	b	50	4242	65
4187	—	4214	5	4243	500 the set
4188	185	4215	85	4244	95
4189	800	4216	45	4245	250
4190	—	4217 a	100	4246	225
4191	40	b	15 ea.	4247 a	165
4192	40	4218	110	b	165
4193	35	4219	38	4248	125
4194	110	4220	200	4249 a	45
4195	50	4221	30 ea.	b	185 with drainer
4196	40	4222	365	c	55
4197	250	4223 a	55	4250	—
4198	—	b	65	4251	350 ea.
4199	20	4224	18	4252	18 ea.
4200 a	25	4225 a	10	4253	30 ea.
b	30	b	15	4254	18 ea.
c	30	c	15	Fig. 19	12 ea. clear wine
d	35	4226 a	10		50 ea. blue wine
e	50	b	10	Fig. 21	12 ea. clear wine
4201	3	4227	45		85 ea. green wine
4202	5	4228	65		
4203	65	4229	10		
4204	20 ea.	4230	10		
4205	65	4231	30		

4255–4260 Decorated by E. J. Swann in Sandwich, but not *manufactured* by Swann.

THREADED GLASS

Objects with colored threads on clear bodies have less value than objects with colored threads on colored bodies. The condition of the threads is critical to the value of the article. Etching and engraving adds to value.

Photo No.

4261	125	blue threads on blue
4262 a	250	ruby threads on clear, engraved
b	85	ruby threads on clear, engraved
4263 a	105	amber threads on amber
b	200	amber threads on amber
4264 a	125 ea.	amber threads on amber, engraved
b	250	amber threads on amber, engraved
4265 a	75	amber threads on amber, engraved
b	250	amber threads on amber, engraved
4266	65	blue threads on clear
4267	85 ea.	ruby threads on clear, needle etched
4268	50 ea.	clear threads on clear, engraved
4269 a	95 ea.	amber threads on amber, engraved
b	75 ea.	ruby threads on clear, engraved
4270	125 ea.	canary threads on canary, needle etched
4271	28 ea.	clear, no threads, engraved
4272	85 ea.	ruby threads on clear, engraved
4273	65 ea.	ruby threads on clear, engraved
4274 a	85 ea.	blue threads on clear
b	115 ea.	canary threads on canary
4275	50	ruby threads on clear, needle etched
4276	50	ruby threads on clear, needle etched
4277	400	ruby threads on clear, engraved
4278	110	ruby threads on clear, engraved
4279	75	ruby threads on clear

Photo No.

4280	200	ruby threads on clear
4281	240	ruby threads on clear
4282	125	ruby threads on clear, cased in white
4283	225	ruby threads on clear
4284	175	ruby threads on clear
4285 a	150 ea.	green threads on green
b	65 ea.	ruby threads on clear
4286	85	ruby threads on clear, etched
4287	65	ruby threads on clear, etched
4288	135	ruby threads on clear, engraved
4289 a	65	white threads on pink
b	95	white threads on pink
c	100	white threads on pink
4290 a	65	white threads on pink
b	95	white threads on pink
c	100	white threads on pink
4291 a	100	white threads on pink
b	150	white threads on orange
4292	95	ruby threads on clear
4293	135	ruby threads on clear
4294	—	
4295 a	35	blue threads on clear
b	135	blue threads on clear

4296	150	green threads on green
4297	140	ruby threads on clear
4298	200	ruby threads on clear
4299	85 the set	canary threads on canary
4300	40	ruby threads on ruby
4301	75 the set	blue-green threads on blue-green
4302	85 the set	ruby threads on clear
4303 a	100 the set	green threads on canary
b	35	ruby threads on blue
4304	85	ruby threads on clear

4305–4320   Decorated by Mary Gregory. Will be priced under *Lighting* and *Salt Shakers*.

EPERGNES

Because it is difficult to find completely assembled epergnes, they command high prices. Individual units and incomplete assemblies do not command high prices. Complete epergnes can be assembled by collecting individual units. The result is financially rewarding.

Photo No.

4321	700	
4322	750	
4323	40	base
	100	Frosted Madonna standard with fittings
	25	trumpet with fitting
	40	center plate
4324	150	Frosted Madonna standard attached to base, with fittings
	25	trumpet with fitting
	40	center plate

Photo No.

4325	300	Frosted Madonna standard attached to base, with fittings and center plate
	25	trumpet with fitting
4326	235	Frosted Madonna standard with fitting
	40	center plate
	300	Frosted Madonna standard attached to center plate, with fittings
	25	trumpet with fitting
4327 a	100	with fittings
b	235	with fitting
4328	—	
4329	10 ea.	
4330	5 ea.	
4331	235	Frosted Madonna standard with fitting, collar
4332	20	
Fig. 28	1000	Fish globe with hooks on standard
	800	Fish globe without hooks on standard
Fig. 29	125	clear
	200 +	color
Fig. 30	4500	with white opal globe
	5000	with blue opal globe
	6500	with lavender opal globe
Fig. 31	2200	
4333	875	

4334 a	150	with fittings
b	40	with fitting
4335	800	
4336	800	
4337	25 ea.	
4338	25	three-hole
	45	six-hole
4339	750	
4340	150	three-unit assembly with fittings
4341	600	
4342	40	
4343	500	
4344	100	with fitting
4345	40	
4346 a	25	with fitting
b	40	with fitting
c	40	with fitting
4347	750	
4348	100	with fitting
4349	875	
4350	100	with fitting
4351	50	with fitting
4352	500	
4353	40 ea.	with fitting
4354 a	65	with fitting
b	35	with fitting
c	50	with fitting
Fig. 32	875	
4355	75	with rod and fitting
4356	200	ruby threads on clear
4357	40	with fitting

SANDWICH CO-OPERATIVE GLASS COMPANY

Photo No.		Photo No.	
4358	500	4370	100
4359	500	4371	1200
4360	225	4372	325 pr.
4361	175	4373	30 ea.
4362	150	4374	125
4363	—	4375	250
4364	110	4376	225
4365	20	4377	225
4366	30	4378	250
4367	90	4379	95
4368	35	4380	165
4369	15	4381	90

TREVAISE

Photo No.

4382	900
4383	—
4384	1200
4385	950
4386	800
4387	600
4388	750
4389	—
4390	800
4391	—